Union

Max Wilkinson

T0246959

methuen | drama

LONDON • NEW YORK • OXFORD • NEW DELHI • SYDNEY

METHUEN DRAMA
Bloomsbury Publishing Plc
50 Bedford Square, London, WC1B 3DP, UK
1385 Broadway, New York, NY 10018, USA
29 Earlsfort Terrace, Dublin 2, Ireland

BLOOMSBURY, METHUEN DRAMA and the Methuen
Drama logo are trademarks of Bloomsbury Publishing Plc

First published in Great Britain 2023

A catalogue record for this book is available from the British Library.

A catalog record for this book is available from the Library of Congress.

ISBN: PB: 978-1-3504-4199-6
ePDF: 978-1-3504-4201-6
eBook: 978-1-3504-4203-0

Series: Modern Plays

Typeset by Mark Heslington Ltd, Scarborough, North Yorkshire

To find out more about our authors and books visit
www.bloomsbury.com and sign up for our newsletters.

Union premiered with a four-week run at Arcola Theatre on 19 July 2023 with the following cast and creative team:

Saskia   **Dominique Tipper**
Dizzy/Leon/Scatter/Fibre/
Lottie/American Sarah/
Dev/Kerry/Mum   **Sorcha Kennedy**
Delroy/Fraser/Lewis/
Toulouse/Sammy/Kade/
Chris Hutton   **Andre Bullock**

Writer Max Wilkinson
Director Wiebke Green
Set & Costume Designer Kit Hinchcliffe
Sound Designer & Composer Julian Starr
Lighting Designer Martha Godfrey
Stage Manager Gwenan Bain
Production Manager Justin Treadwell
PR Mobius
Marketing & Communications Velenzia Spearpoint
Videographer Rich Rusk Films
Project Manager Maeve O'Neill
Co-producers Rua Arts, Anarchy Division, Velenzia Spearpoint & Max Wilkinson

DOMINIQUE TIPPER – Saskia

Dominique can most recently be seen as British intelligence officer Smith opposite Thomas Jane and John Malvovich in Lionsgate's action feature *One Ranger*. And in 2022 she played Kelly in the TV miniseries adaptation of the feature film *Headhunters*. 2021 saw her return for the sixth and final season of Amazon Prime's critically acclaimed series *The Expanse* in the lead role of Naomi Nagata, based on the popular sci-fi novels by James S.A. Corey. Dominique's other film credits include *Monday*, alongside Sebastian Stan and Denise Gough, *The Girl with All the Gifts*, with Gemma Arterton, Glenn Close and Paddy Considine, and *Fast Girls*, with Lily James. She has also featured in Warner Bros.'s *Fantastic Beasts and Where to Find Them* and Mark Waters's adaptation of Richelle Mead's *Vampire Academy*. In 2018 Dominique directed and produced her first short film *Trying to Find Me*, based on the one-woman play of the same name. And at the end of the same year, Dominique conceptualised, produced and directed her first music video for 'Egos' by up-and-coming East London rapper SmoothVee. https://theartistspartnership.co.uk/artist/dominique-tipper/ Instagram: @MissTipper

SORCHA KENNEDY – Dizzy/Leon/Scatter/Fibre/Lottie/American Sarah/Dev/Kerry/Mum

Theatre credits include: *Contractions* (Omnibus Theatre), *Rainer* (Arcola Theatre – nominated for Lead Performance in a Play in Offie Awards 2022), *Diary of a Somebody* (Seven Dials Playhouse), Sam Wanamaker Festival (Shakespeare's Globe), *Humbug!* (Citizens Theatre/Tramway, Glasgow), and *A Midsummer Night's Dream*, *The Comedy of Errors* (PSF). Radio credits include: *The Nazis: Rise to Power* (BBC Radio 4) and *Whenever I Get Blown Up I Think of You* (BBC Radio Scotland/RCS). Sorcha trained at the Royal Conservatoire of Scotland where she was awarded the Citizens Theatre Society Award. She is also a filmmaker and visual artist. Her debut film,

Sisyphos, screened at numerous Academy Award and BAFTA-qualifying film festivals, receiving various nominations and awards in 2022. *sorcha-kennedy.com/*

ANDRE BULLOCK – Delroy/Fraser/Lewis/Toulouse/Sammy/Kade/Chris Hutton

Andre trained at Drama Studio London. His theatre credits include *As You Like It* (C Theatre, Edinburgh Fringe), *The Talented Mr Ripley* (The Faction) and *Sincere as Objects* (Volcano Theatre). TV and film include *Maleficent: Mistress of Evil* (Disney), *Casualty* (BBC) and *Sandman* (Netflix). Radio includes *A Passage to India* (BBC Radio 4) and *Iron Anthology – Ore* (Via Brooklyn). Instagram: @andre_bullock

MAX WILKINSON – Writer

Max is an award-winning playwright and screenwriter, fascinated with characters trying to navigate an increasingly absurd world. He has won the Screen to Screen Award, the Paris Prix and was a finalist for the Nick Darke Award, Theatre Uncut's Political Playwriting Award, Samuel French's Off-Broadway Awards and was recently nominated for an Off West Award. He has had work staged at Theatre503, Arcola Theatre, Paines Plough, King's Head Theatre and many others. He is currently under commission by Pennway Productions for his first large budget feature film *Ghost Fruit* and by BBC Radio 4 for his play *Rainer*, published by Methuen Drama. He teaches screenwriting at the Met Film School, on their BA course. maxwilkinson-theatre.com/ Instagram: @maxwilkinson_

WIEBKE GREEN – Director

Wiebke recently directed the *New York Times* Critics' Pick and OffWestEnd OnComm winner *The Poltergeist* by Philip Ridley at the Arcola Theatre. Direction includes *The Journey to Venice* (Finborough Theatre), *Tarantula* (Southwark Playhouse), *The*

Beast Will Rise (online series for Tramp Productions), *Sadness and Joy in the Life of Giraffes* (Orange Tree Theatre), *This Might Not Be It* (R&D project with Bush Theatre and Broccoli Arts) and *Everybody Cares, Everybody Understands* (Vault Festival). She trained at the Orange Tree Theatre with an MA in Theatre Directing, and as intern director to Katie Mitchell on *Orlando* (Schaubühne, Berlin) and *Anatomie eines Suizids* (Schauspielhaus, Hamburg). Assistant direction includes *Scrounger* (Finborough Theatre), *Dealing with Clair* (Orange Tree Theatre), *The Beast of Blue Yonder* (ArtsEd), *The Frontier Trilogy* and *Sirenia* (Edinburgh Fringe). Her work with drama schools includes *In the Forest of Starlight* and *Shrapnel* (Royal Welsh College of Music & Drama/Yard Theatre), *Heather's Wedding* as a guest director for Mountview's Catalyst Festival (Theatre503), *As You Like It*, *Julius Caesar* and *Cannibals* (London School of Dramatic Art). Instagram/Twitter: @WiebkeGreen

KIT HINCHCLIFFE – Set & Costume Designer

Kit trained at Central St Martin's College of Art and Design. Since graduating, her work has spanned theatre, dance and installation. She is Co-Artistic Director of Lidless Theatre and regularly collaborates with Architecture Social Club as Designer/Fabricator. Work includes: *Leaves of Glass* (Park Theatre), *Oresteia* (Corbett Theatre), *The Journey to Venice* (Finborough Theatre), *The Poltergeist* (Arcola), *Camino Real and Cymbeline* (Bridewell Theatre), *Mapping Gender* (Baltic Centre for Contemporary Art/Cambridge Junction/The Place), *A Hideous Monstrous Verminous Creature* (The Place), *La Bohème* (King's Head Theatre), *Boys* (Barbican Centre), *Festen* (Corbett Theatre), *Tender Napalm* (King's Head Theatre), *Well Lit* (Dansstationen Malmö/The Place), *Moonfleece* (Pleasance Theatre), *Pebbles* (Katzpace), *Heroes* (Bridge House Theatre), *Beetles from the West* (Hope Theatre) and *Fundamentals* (Platform TheatreKX). Instagram: @kit_hinchcliffe

JULIAN STARR – Sound Designer & Composer

Julian's recent sound design work in the UK includes *Song from Far Away* (HOME Manchester/Hampstead Theatre), *ZOG* (West End/UK tour), *Rose* (Hope Mill/Park Theatre/ Ambassadors Theatre – Offie nominated for Best Sound Design), *Animal* (Park Theatre/UK tour), *Never Not Once*, *Cry Havoc*, *Martha and Josie and the Chinese Elvis* (all Park Theatre); *Lesbian Space Crimes*, *You Only Live Forever* (both Soho Theatre), *Sleepwalking* (Hampstead Theatre), *How to Survive an Apocalypse*, *Scrounger* (Offie nomination for Best Sound Design) and *The Wind of Heaven* (all Finborough Theatre), *The Dwarfs* (White Bear Theatre – Offie nomination for Best Sound Design) and *Aisha* (Tristan Bates Theatre – Offie nomination for Best Sound Design). Recent sound design work in Australia includes *Return to the Dirt* (Queensland Theatre Company), *Elektra/Orestes* (Brisbane Metro Arts – Blue Curtains Award for Best Sound Design), *Miss Peony* (Belvoir Street Theatre) and *Hyperdream* (Sydney Theatre Award for Best Sound Design). Site-specific production work includes *The Comedy of Errors*, *Pericles* (Valtice Castle, Czech Republic), King's Head Theatre's 50th birthday celebrations and *The Third* (Victoria & Albert Museum). Media and television work includes Fizzy Sherbet podcast, *White Tuesday* (Sarah Awards Best Audio Fiction) and *Bluey* (as Music Editor for BBC/ABC/Disney). Julian is the Associate Sound Designer at the Finborough Theatre. He worked as a touring sound engineer for *An Inspector Calls* (UK/Ireland tour) and as a sound engineer for *Songs for Nobodies* (Ambassadors Theatre) and *The Tap Pack* (Peacock Theatre). julianstarrsound.com | Twitter: @JulianStarr15 | Instagram: @julianstarr94

MARTHA GODFREY – Lighting Designer

Martha is a lighting and projection designer working across theatre, dance, musicals and live art. Past work includes *Sugar Coat* (Southwark Playhouse), *Flies* (Shoreditch Town

Hall), *Much Ado (The Remix)* (National Youth Theatre/Duke of York's Theatre), *The Prince* (Southwark Playhouse), *Mapping Gender* (UK tour/The Place), *Bangers* (UK tour/Soho Theatre), *But I'm a Cheerleader* (Turbine Theatre), *Passion Fruit* (New Diorama Theatre), *Home, I'm Darling* (Theatre Royal, Bury St Edmunds), *Oliver Twist!* (Chester Storyhouse), *What Do You See* (Shoreditch Town Hall), *Redemption* (The Big House), *Pink Lemonade* (Bush Theatre), *Concrete Jungle Book* (Pleasance Theatre), *Fever Pitch* (Hope Theatre), *Around the World in Eighty Days* (Theatre Royal, Bury St Edmunds), *Time and Tide* (Park Theatre), *Before I Was a Bear* (The Bunker), *I Wanna Be Yours* (UK tour/Bush Theatre), *Unknown Rivers* (Hampstead Downstairs), *We Dig* (Ovalhouse), *Cabildo* (Arcola Theatre), *GREY* (Ovalhouse), *WHITE* (Ovalhouse/ Pleasance at Edinburgh Fringe/UK tour), *Exceptional Promise* (Bush Theatre), *Fuck You Pay Me* (The Bunker/Rich Mix/ Assembly Rooms, Edinburgh Fringe/Vaults Festival). marthagodfrey.co.uk | Twitter: @MarthaGodfrey2

Union

Characters

Saskia, *never stops smiling, despite dying on the inside. She is good-looking, slim, athletic, funny, charming and successful but, as the play progresses, she cannot hide her inherent eccentricity and tragedy.*

Dizzy
Delroy
Leon
Fraser
Scatter
Lewis
Toulouse
Fibre
Sammy
Lottie
American Sarah
Dev
Kade
Kerry
Chris Hutton
Mum

Note

With characters named, such as **Dizzy**, **Leon**, **Fraser** *and all the others* **Saskia** *meets, these people appear physically whereas when Saskia recalls scenes and other characters, with their speech in quotation marks, it means they do not appear physically and are only described by Saskia with their speech imitated by her too.*

However, this is just a projection and proposal. Each production can make up it's own mind and experiment with who says what. For example, they may wish all the named characters as well as the speech in quote marks to also be performed by other actors or, as indicated, have **Saskia** *read these parts. That's up to them.*

Casting

This play should ideally be performed by three actors, with one actor playing the lead role exclusively and the other two multi-roling the other characters. If the production chose, they could even have one performer treat this as a one-person show and perform all the voices themselves.

Again, multi-roling is up to the production but if using three performers, I would recommend:

Performer one: just plays **Saskia**.

Performer two: **Dizzy**, **Scatter**, **Fibre**, **Lottie**, **Dev**, **Kerry**, **Mum**, **Leon**, **American Sarah**.

Performer three: **Delroy**, **Fraser**, **Lewis**, **Toulouse**, **Sammy**, **Kade**, **Hip Ed**, **Chris**.

Style

The script jumps between the canal, memories and phone calls with characters entering as well as Saskia describing them. But, with all the changes, Saskia's narration remains throughout to guide the reader through.

Staging

Given the nature of the fast character changes and constant movement of the scenes and action, a Brechtian style of exposed costumes on stage and costume changes is suggested.

Design

Rather than lavish complicated sets, and given the nature in which the play moves and scenes change, a simple but movable set is suggested, with theatrical creativity in terms of staging rather than a solid single set – generally relying more on strong lights, an immersive soundtrack and changing costumes to tell this story. But again, it is up to the production company or director.

A warm summer's evening in Westbourne Park, near Portobello Road, London, on the Grand Union Canal.

The moonlight is laid out on the still, black water like a mosaic.

Thick branches of trees lay heavy in the darkness.

It is midsummer and there is distant music to the west.

Except for that, only the occasional croak from the water or rustle from the bush can be heard.

There is a bench too where there is a strange shadowy mass.

We hear a phone ringing and someone approach.

Saskia *enters from the east, from brand new towers in the distance.*

She's a woman in her thirties, slim and wearing lycra jogging gear with

discreet, state-of-the-art headphones

and her phone attached to her waist.

Her phone keeps on ringing as

she punches and leaps across the air

and rolls on the ground and

runs back and forth.

She finally rejects the call and, smiling, stands and faces us,

but then continues to move around as she speaks:

Saskia (*to audience*)   Smell that.

That's the city. In all it's hurling, blurring glory.

Sweet, summered,

and partly asleep.

But sick, too . . .

and angry.

Angry with me . . .

And all of you.

And let me tell you, tonight:

. . . one of us is going to die.

. . . But not now, that's later. For now picture this:

The Grand Union Canal,

pebble stoned and

moon mosaic-ed on water,

trees all thick with croaking night.

slipping, sleepily through Park Royal,

where I work.

Eckerd and Wise, you might have heard of us?

We might have built your flat.

But now we're building a city . . .

A whole universe in those old estates.

And then I finish up and jog down here, take the tube at Portobello.

She shows off her lycra suit and her body:

And look, I got all the kit:

The best lycra money can buy.

Streamlined fitting. Little pocket for your cards.

Keeps everything in order.

All your bits . . .

Keeps your fanny in,

know what I mean?

This kit is anti-fanny fall-out!

But not that I need that.

Cos look at me.

Like polished oak.

And at thirty-four things should be sagging, right?

Slight droop of the arse. Tits gone a bit crap.

An inevitable decline. Like the melting of the ice-caps.

But not me, sister.

Look at those calves. Straight and true like extractor blades.

She pulls up her top to reveal her stomach. She looks at a member of the audience.

I mean look at my stomach, madam.

Look at it.

You could eat an egg off that.

Now.

Look at yours.

Yeah. Think about it.

But no, I'm not here to belittle you. We can't all be aerodynamic.

We can't all afford the gear.

Some of us prefer to fart it out on sweaty Saturdays with American Sarah

and the other yoga mums.

Not I, though.

I like it out here.

You can smell the river here.

Musty, green, croaking darkness.

Moon mosaic-ed on its surface –

Stop.

. . . Said that. Said that before.

My brain's being doing that recently.

Running away with itself.

know what I mean?

. . . and . . .

I've been having dreams . . .

Suddenly, someone wearing white runs past in the trees, laughing.

But just as they appear, they disappear.

Saskia *looks to this fearfully . . .*

. . . I think it's the situation in Ukraine.

. . .

I think the situation in Ukraine is firing up my brain.

Her phone rings again.

She rejects the call.

. . .

But not tonight.

Tonight, I got to be top-tip.

No, mistakes.

Tonight's the night.

Tonight's the . . .

. . . There's the tube.

Same as ever.

Just got to take it.

But . . .

Maybe I'll . . . sit.

Yeah. Sit for a bit . . . on the bushy, trash-bag-covered bench . . .

She sits down on a bench behind her and looks up at the moon.

She jumps up immediately though as there is a scream behind her.

A man is sitting there, obscured in the dark. He is drinking a can of cider and eating from a box of grapes.

Delroy   AHH!

Saskia (*to audience*)   But the bench erupts!

(*To* **Delroy**.) AH! Fuck. Sorry. I –

Delroy   What you doin'? –

Saskia   Sorry, I thought you were a . . . a bag.

Delroy   A bag?!

Saskia   It's the strikes, there's trash everywhere! I'm sorry, look –

She goes through her pockets to find some change.

Delroy   I'm not homeless!

Bloody hell, can't a man sit somewhere these days without being accused of being homeless or bag-like –

Saskia   Look, I'm sorry, OK? I'm sorry.

She attempts to leave but damages her foot in the process. She winces with pain and then sits beside **Delroy** *rubbing her foot.* **Delroy** *takes out a can of cheap cider.*

Delroy   Sit down, take it easy.

. . . What you doing here, anyway? You some kind of serial killer?

Saskia   No, I'm . . . – I work here. Well, in Park Royal.

Delroy   That's a dump.

Saskia   Well, not anymore. I'm a developer? With Eckerd and Wise?

Delroy   . . . I see.

Saskia   Yeah, we're building a city there. With HS2 and everything. A whole new city.

Delroy (*bitterly*)   I know what you're doing, I've read the pamphlets.

(*Beat.*)

Saskia   In fact we've signed the deal tonight. Having a big party back at mine to celebrate –

Delroy   So why you here talking to me? Why aren't you there, with your friends?

Saskia *looks to the trees. She inhales slowly.* **Delroy** *is surprised.*

Delroy   . . . you OK?

Saskia   . . . I don't know. I just feel a little off.

Saskia *breathes strangely and regains composure.* **Delroy** *looks concerned.*

Delroy   This is too weird. It's like having a drink your abuser. Or Phillip Schofield.

Saskia   You're not fans of us then?

Delroy   You're not fans of me! £8.95 for a pint of Guinness at the Cow now, £8.95.

Saskia *smiles.*

Delroy   They used to have music there too. Used to be music everywhere.

Saskia   You from round here then?

Delroy   Used to, before the rents went insane. I come back sometimes, to have a look around.

Saskia   It's lovely here though, isn't it? Meanwhile Gardens.

Delroy   Oh yeah, you know how it got that name, Meanwhile Gardens.

Saskia   How?

Delroy   Well, after World War 2 it was a bomb-site. So all these people from the community they wanted to turn it into a park. So, they begged the council. And the council said they would but they did nothing. For years. So meanwhile, the community, they did it themselves. Built the park. The allotment. The skate park. The woods. So they called it Meanwhile.

Saskia   That's lovely.

Delroy   Yeah, shame it's all fucked.

Saskia   What?

Her breathing gets worse.

Delroy   Oh, come on, you know. You lot did it.

Saskia   I don't know.

Delroy   They're turning it into a car park. Tearing up the trees, tearing up Trellick Tower. And all these gardens.

Saskia   No!

Delroy   My mate just told me. We pushed you lot out in 2003, then again in 2009 but you never give up, come on.

Saskia   . . .

Delroy   I'd be angry if I wasn't so incredibly drunk. But that's how it always goes. You lot always win.

Saskia's *breathing becomes strained again.*

Saskia   Who's developing the land?

Delroy   Morley Estates.

Saskia   Hah, Morley! They couldn't piss in a kettle, you'll be fine. And just for the record, we are not Morley Estates. They're scum, they're –

Suddenly, in the trees, a teenage girl, **Dizzy***, in a white summer's dress runs through the bushes, laughing.*

She runs through and disappears.

Again, only **Saskia** *notices her.* **Delroy** *looks at her, concerned.*

Saskia   Me and my mate, Dizzy . . . we came down here once. This day in May but it was baking hot. To buy all this weed in Portobello.

Then we couldn't afford the train back so we walked all the way home along the canal, to Stratford.

But we never made it home . . .

Delroy   Why?

Saskia   . . . we got caught on Hackney Marshes . . .

She doesn't hear him, but stares into the distance. She has an idea, like a revelation.

. . . But I could do it now.

She checks her smart watch: looking at the map. And stretching her limbs.

Delroy   What?

Saskia   I could run all the way home! I could run home . . . finish the journey.

Delroy   But that . . . that's miles?

Saskia   Well, maybe for you my bag-like friend but I have actually run a half marathon in Brighton. Plus a 10k in Fife.

Delroy   But what if you . . . get mugged? You look like a walking Apple Store.

What if you fall in?

Saskia (*stretching still*)   Well, that would be bad cos I can't swim.

Delroy   . . . Are you OK?

Saskia   Course I'm OK!

Course I'm OK. This is the best I've felt years. This is exactly what I need!

I swear I'd kiss you if you weren't so grubby! – Sorry –

Delroy   Wait! WAIT!

But **Saskia** *runs away, excitedly, east along the canal as* **Delroy** *shouts after her then disappears.*

Saskia (*to audience*)   Wait? Wait!

Why I am gonna wait!

This is the best idea since sliced bread!

Since . . . since . . . – Tony Blair!

I need an adventure. To see something green.

But first a tune to see me through . . .

She presses her smart watch: a disco tune comes on, one she loves.

She dances to the music while jogging and speaking.

Yes!

Old school!

That will do.

A disco banger down memory lane.

There's the Westway, swinging right.

And Trellick Tower, looming down.

And . . .

Dizzy, *the girl in the white dress, runs through again, laughing.*

Saskia's *smart watch rings; she doesn't notice.*

Saskia   Dizzy!

(*To audience.*) 'Come on!' running through!

We were Thelma and Louise!

Bonnie and Clyde,

Just with less suicide.

. . . Well . . .

. . .

ring ring . . .

Dizzy *disappears.*

Saskia *notices her phone:*

She looks at the screen and smiles, answering it and still running.

Saskia   Hi, babe. How are you?

Leon   Saskia?! Saskia? What's going on? Fraser said you ran out the meeting, he's pissing blood.

Saskia   It's sorted, it's fine. How's the party?

Leon   . . . Horrible. They're all early. Rosa's crying. Are you at the big Sainsbury's?

Saskia   Um . . .

Leon   Are you at the little Waitrose?

Saskia   . . . Um. Babe, I'm . . . taking a tiny detour.

Leon   What?

Saskia   I'm running home. Along the Grand Union Canal.

Leon   . . .

Saskia   It's fine, it's only actually gonna add a tiny bit more time –

Leon   SASKIA! The Ocado has not come!

Saskia   What?

Leon (*breaking down*)   . . . The. Ocado. Has not come . . .

Saskia   Look, Leon. In the airing cupboard. There is a
secret quiche. Take it out –

Leon   This is not about quiche! This is about . . . now.
About you. About last night, about the whole year, about –

Saskia *rejects the call angrily.*

Then she looks at the audience and smiles.

Saskia (*to audience*)   God, my husband Leon. Love him to
bits he is such a pussy.

Massive cock though.

It's always the quiet ones.

Anyway . . .

where are we?

Concrete paths.

Green falls away, little bleak, but opens up to . . .

. . . Yes!

King's Cross!

Floating bars and luxury flats in old gas works.

We did some of this! Eckerd and Wise.

One of my first jobs, actually.

Those estates over there.

Shakespeare Estate. Built a community centre, the Globe . . .

God, I remember that first day,

Groped in the lift. Lynx Africa breath.

Then crammed in a boardroom with twenty big dicks.

She imagines that first day with her boss, **Fraser***, who goes over plans for a new development.*

Pouring over maps of Birmingham,

Liverpool,

Clacton-on-Sea!

'Where there's shit, there's a way!'

said Fraser, my boss. As I stood all quiet and wide-eyed at the back.

Empty depots, docks, the old Safeways.

Knock it down, fill them up.

With steel and glass.

Posh flats and Pure Gyms.

Restaurants and burger joints.

Clubs and swimming pools up in the sky.

Carve it up, rip it out.

But. If the building was really nice, you know, old and spicy.

Keep the frame, keep the features.

Force steel rods down rotting timber.

Fuck the tower, keep the clock.

The old workhouse become a pizza-stop.

The naval base, a pastry shop.

And the old factory, where men and women used their hands.

Where machines picked and clanged.

And the brass band played on Tuesday nights.

That would be a shopping mall.

A disco-tech. A craft ale mausoleum.

And the old estates: we ripped them out like bad teeth.

And made new homes, that bloomed and bloomed.

I didn't hear him call . . . –

'Saskia!'

Saskia *jumps awake from her daydream, back in the meeting with* **Fraser**.

'Yeah?'

'It is Saskia, isn't it?'

. . . I don't know why he singled me out that day, but he did.

Me all mousy and weird at the back.

'What do you think?'

he said, pointing to a map of King's Cross.

'I think it looks . . . nice.'

'Thank you, Saskia. But what do we do about the locals?'

Um.

'They don't like it.'

'. . . Why?'

'Cos they're silly, and stupid, and sentimental.'

They'd rather see it all to waste.

They dream of whistle blows and marching bands.

Of factory strikes and coal-black hands.

'I see.'

Now, if we just tear all this down. We'll have a mutiny on our hands.

First petitions.

Then local press.

Then the crusties come in.

'Oh, they're the worst!'

Patchouli-ed and billboarded and singing their chants!

'Oh, Jeremy Corbyn! Oh, Jeremy –'

Saskia   No!

. . .

Now, like Fraser put it: the flats, they were gonna go up either way!

We just had to find a route that was a little more humane.

And anything to get those chants out of our ears.

. . .

'I know! We'll make something for them!'

And I realised I had a knack for it.

Pop in a pool, a community library.

'How'd you like to extend uni campus from King's Cross to Highbury?'

Just like now, with Park Royal, and the West!

Those tenancy groups, the Union Collective: they'd melt like butter in my buttery hands.

'A community theatre, madam? Why bloody not!'

The placards came down,

the chants, they all ceased.

Her breathing becomes more agitated again; she has palpitations.

'If you need someone, to sort out your crap,

Saskia here,

she's got the knack!'

. . . A people's person.

Imagine, me!

Little old Sask, with bloodied-up knees. The loser, the nerd.
The bookworm, the freak . . .

could pour her creativity, her *soul* into this work!

Finally they could see,

that I was good,

good for something . . .

me . . .

Me . . .

ME! –

STOP!

She can't breathe and has to stop.

She looks around. She's lost.

So, why tonight. Do I feel so bad?

. . .

. . . But where am I now?

Council blocks shiver up.

Canal falls away . . .

Estates . . . wait . . . I know this place –

. . . phone rings again.

Oh dear.

She answers her phone; it's **Fraser**.

She's all smiles again.

Saskia   Fraser, babes. Was just thinking about you . . . – I think I'm at the Shakespeare Estates, you know where we did that youth centre, the Globe?

Fraser   . . .

Saskia   . . . Anyway, how are you?

Fraser   . . . how am I? How am I, she asks.

Saskia   . . . Fraser –

Fraser   I'LL TELL YOU HOW I FUCKING AM, SASK –

I'm standing in a room with the board, the foreman, that Union Collective –

Saskia   Yes –

Fraser   The Mayor of Brentford and about a thousand sandwiches!

Saskia   Fraser –

Fraser   I have never seen a mayor eat a ploughman's so aggressively. And I've had lunch with Sadiq Khan.

Saskia   Fraser –

Fraser   And just as we are about to sign the biggest contract for the biggest new development in Europe, possibly the WORLD –

Saskia   Frase –

Fraser   My project manager runs away!

Saskia   . . . I did not run away –

Fraser   You literally ran away! They saw you at reception. In your little shorts.

Saskia   I just thought. You didn't need me –

Fraser   Of course we need you! The Union Collective, that tenancy association, those mums and vicars, those local types

– you know they won't sign without you. And we can't sign without them!

Saskia   . . .

Fraser   You sold them this deal, Sask. The Union Collective. You.

Saskia   I know.

Fraser   Where are you?

Saskia   . . . Angel. My phone's about to die, but –

Fraser   Get back now –

Saskia   But Fraser –

Fraser   If you don't get back right now that's it.

Saskia *notices two people approach her from the dark council estates.*

Saskia (*to audience*)   Shit.

Fraser   Saskia?

Saskia (*to audience*)   From the dark estates, two boys in hoods slip down from the gravel walls –

Scatter   Oi, miss,

Saskia (*to audience*)   Two wolves, Romulus and Remus, as I reject the call –

Fraser   SASKIA?!

Saskia*'s eyes widen though as she sees something move in the dark estates.*

Two teenage boys, **Scatter** *and* **Lewis***, enter. Working-class,*

London accents. **Scatter** *wears a hoody and holds a tiny speaker playing 'Protein' by Jeshi, feat. Obongjayar.*

Scatter   What phone is that?

Saskia   . . .

Lewis   You alright, miss? Cos you look kind of nuts, muttering to yourself.

Scatter *reaches for something in his pocket.*

Saskia   Oi! I warn you, yeah. I know Krav Maga.

Scatter   What the fuck is Krav Maga? Like yoga?

Saskia   No, it's an Israeli martial art. It's incredibly powerful.

Lewis   Yeah, it's like aggy yoga. They do it up at the Globe.

Scatter (*laughing*)   Seen.

Saskia   Look, I haven't got a phone!

Her phone/smart watch starts ringing.

Fuck.

Scatter   It's one of them smart watches, innit.

The boys laugh.

Saskia   Why do you care?

Scatter   Cos we want it and then we gonna dump you in the canal.

Lewis (*to* **Scatter**)   Shut up.

(*To* **Saskia**.) We don't want your phone. We want chip . . . Tobacco?

Saskia   What for?

Scatter *takes the thing out of his pocket: it's a bag of weed.*

Scatter   For a spliff, bruv! Lemon Diesel, Stinky Weasel. Paint my easel –

Lewis   Don't spit man, you're bare shit.

(*To* **Saskia**.) We got cash. Just need someone to get it.

Saskia (*to audience*)   He takes a twenty-pound note. My watch rings again. Fraser, FUCK!

I turn back to them.

Saskia   Look, where's the tube?

Scatter   They're on strike.

Saskia   Fuck. I'll get an Uber –

Lewis   They're on strike too, my brothers one.

Saskia   Fuck! OK, listen: you take me to a cab-rank, yeah? I'll get you your cancer sticks.

Lewis   . . . Cool.

Lewis *and* **Scatter** *lead her through the estates and through a busy main road.*

Saskia (*to audience*)   They lead me up sloping road,

past scraggy trees to Upper Street,

to the corner shop and cabs nearby.

Where I buy them a twenty pack of Pall Malls.

And sit about and roll a spliff.

'Protein' by Jeshi, feat. Obongjayar plays. **Lewis** *rolls a spliff quickly as* **Scatter** *dances to the music.*

Saskia   . . . Did you boys say you were from the Shakespeare Estate? You know the Globe?

Lewis   . . . Yeah? Why?

Saskia   We developed it, my company. How is it?

Lewis *shrugs.*

Scatter   I like it. I like that little cafe in the Globe. I like them little gluten-free cupcakes they do.

Lewis (*kisses teeth*)   When do you ever go in there?

Scatter   All the time, bruv: man's got a gluten intolerance.

Lewis   Fuck you have.

Scatter   Why do you think I get so heavy after bread?

Lewis *tuts.*

Scatter   And I like that little new park. I like to watch them young mums do their squats. Booyah!

Lewis   Bruv, when do you go in the park? They build the estate around us so we can't even get in. You can't afford the Globe, you can't afford the cakes. They cross the street when you pass by.

Scatter   . . .

Saskia   Less crime, though?

Lewis   Well, there's less people so there's less crime. It's a ghost town.

Saskia   . . .

Scatter   Why do you care? You're leaving –

Lewis   Nah –

Saskia   Where you going?

Scatter   . . . Uni, innit.

Lewis   But I ain't going.

Saskia   No, you have to go. I never went and I still regret it.

Lewis *hands her the spliff.* **Saskia** *takes it, smoking absent-mindedly*

Lewis   What were you gonna do?

Saskia   English Lit. I used to love writing. I won a prize in a magazine for my story when I was ten and Dad put it up on the fridge. But when he left Mum took it down.

I used to come down on the canal, but back in the east, where I live. When they were tearing each other apart. And then me and my mate Dizzy, all we did was read, and smoke weed. And once we walked all the way home along here. Quoting *On the Road* and . . . and *Robinson Crusoe* and the *Odyssey*, and all that.

Scatter   Bruv, that's moist.

Saskia (*laughing*)   Yes, it was very moist . . . but Dizzy didn't care. She was always getting beat up at school.

'Oi, big-head', they'd get right in her face, 'why is your head so big, is it cos you're a lesbian?'

The boys laugh.

She once told Shanice Lane to fuck off by the chicken shop . . . she was my hero, she didn't even know it . . .

Lewis   What happened to her?

Saskia   . . .

Lewis *points across the quiet street.*

Scatter   Well, it's over there, miss, if you want to reminisce.

Saskia   What?

Scatter   The canal, it starts again, over there.

Saskia (*to audience*)   . . . And sure enough . . .

there it was.

Great green door to Olympus.

Pebble-dash path,

Sneaking down to ivy-soaked

lungs.

She stands and walks towards the canal in a reverie, holding the spliff.

Lewis   Miss?

Dizzy *appears in her white dress, smiling. Again, only* **Saskia** *sees her.*

Dizzy *goes running off into the trees.* **Saskia** *runs after her.* **Scatter** *and* **Lewis** *call after her. They disappear.*

Saskia (*to audience*)   And we sat here, me and her,

Lewis   Miss, what you doin'?

Saskia (*to audience*)   blue sky and gold water.

. . . before launching off.

'Come on!'

She shouted as we ran into the trees –

the boys shout but I'm off, I'm off, with Dizzy!

Lewis   MISS!

Scatter   Oi, bruv, she's got the weed!

Saskia (*to audience*)   Launching down the canal,

'Come on!'

To Haggerston,

The Island Queen,

to the future.

'Come on!'

'Wait, Dizzy, wait . . .'

A bird is heard calling, in the present.

But as she disappears,

in the dark, there's a flash.

The bird tweets again.

and out the bushes comes a beautiful white bird,

a heron, or something,

with black streaks.

And extends it's wings like Athena.

and glides across the black water.

Flying home,

flying east . . .

Dizzy . . .

Saskia's *smart watch rings again. She smiles and, still running, answers the call.*

She thinks it's **Leon**.

Saskia   Listen babe, when I get back I promise you at least three very good blowjobs –

Leon   Fraser's here.

Saskia   . . . What?

Leon   He said everyone left the meeting, everyone signed except for the tenant's association, the Union Collective they said they won't sign without you.

Saskia   Fuck.

Leon   And . . .

Saskia   What?

Leon   American Sarah's here too.

Saskia   Why?

Leon   Because I invited her –

Saskia   So disinvite her.

Leon   How?

Saskia   I don't know. Tell her I'm having a wanking fit. Or we've got asbestos.

Leon   But why?

Saskia   Because she's boring and basic and for some reason she smells like yeast.

Leon   She's got a condition!

Saskia   I don't care! She's a whiney little bread-head.

Leon   What?

Saskia   Do you want to fuck her? Is that it? Do you want to fuck American Sourdough?

Leon   It's because she talks to me, Saskia, she talks to me.

Saskia   . . .

Leon   Anyway, what about you and Fraser?

Saskia   Oh, come on –

Leon   It doesn't matter –

Saskia   No, it doesn't –

Saskia   Leon, there's –

Leon   Listen.

He sighs.

Saskia   . . .?

Leon   I was binning some stuff in the kitchen and my keys dropped in the bin –

Saskia   I see –

Leon   I found those pills, Sask. All those empty aspirin packets . . . –

The smart watch bleeps as it runs out of battery. **Saskia** *can't hear him as much as it does so.*

Saskia   I had a migraine –

Leon   There was tons of them, Saskia. All empty.

Saskia   . . .

Leon   That's why you were like that that weekend, when I got back? Just . . . dead. Staring at the walls. And I found your clothes all muddy and wet.

Saskia   . . . No.

Leon   You'd been out on Hackney Marshes, hadn't you?

Saskia's *smart-watch bleeps as it is running out of battery.*

Saskia   . . . wait, Leon –

Leon   Saskia, listen. I love you. But I can't help you. I can't help you if you don't tell me what's going on!

Saskia   Leon!

Leon   Sask –

Her smart watch runs out of battery. She screams and kicks the ground.

Fuck! Shit.

She starts to run eastward.

(*To audience.*) FUCK!

Come on, Sask. Come on.

. . .

She hears laughter, sees lights. A glow on her face as she smiles.

Hold on . . .

Trendy people, drooped across bridges,

drinking Rebellion beers. Bikes ride by,

Dutch as fuck.

And in a nearby loft, its doors open to the canal,

some DM-ed beauties gyrate and twist,

in the throbbing air.

In an artist's loft, open to the canal, trendy artist people dance to a sound system and have a party. They listen to house music.

Toulouse *is a very tall, broad, shaven-headed man in latex boots and a tank top; he has an American accent and wears make-up.*

Fibre *is dressed more like an activist, but a trendy one: short cropped hair, DM boots, baggy shirt. She's British.*

Toulouse (*singing to the song*)   'Dress it, bitch, dress it, bitch; dress it, dress it, dress it, bitch!'

Saskia   Hello, hi? Can you tell me where we are?

Fibre   . . . Er . . . Dalston?

They turn down music.

Saskia   Oh, thank God . . . listen, you don't happen to have a charger for a smart watch, do you? Like I need to make some calls, like right now. Like it's an emergency.

Fibre   . . . Um, I'll have a look?

She takes her smart watch and exits into the party.

Toulouse   You OK, babes?

Saskia   Yeah. Sure – have you ever fucked up your entire life in one fell swoop?

Toulouse   . . . Um –

Saskia   Look, don't listen to me. I'm just some river hag –

Toulouse   Babe. Share.

He hands **Saskia** *her drink.*

Saskia   . . . So, tonight, right, I had the biggest meeting of my career and I literally . . . ran away. Down the canal.

Toulouse   Why?

Saskia   Because I couldn't physically open the door. I was gonna puke. I . . . –

. . .

(*Still shaking*.) Do you ever . . . do you ever feel . . .

like you're dissolving? Like you're just melting into thin air?

Like this life you've built around you is just . . . collapsing.

Toulouse (*pensively*)   Yeah . . . sure.

. . . Every time I do ketamine. Do you want some?

He offers her a tube from around his neck. **Fibre** *returns.*

Saskia   God, no! . . . – I mean if it was coke.

Fibre   We have coke.

Saskia   . . . Well, still, no. I promised my husband. And this counsellor. And a Crown Court.

Fibre   So, what do you do?

Saskia   I'm a developer.

Fibre *freezes.*

Toulouse   Oh, wow.

Saskia   Yeah, we're developing Park Royal, in the west.

Toulouse   Oh my God, that brand new city?

Saskia   . . . Yeah.

Toulouse   You've got that new gallery, right? X Gallery?

Fibre *tuts.*

Saskia   Sure. But we need a curator –

Toulouse   Oh my God! Are you fucking kidding? This is what I do, bitch!

Saskia   Well . . . come in, come in.

Toulouse   Fucking hell, yeah! And *you* should be celebrating!

Saskia   . . . . I *should* be celebrating.

Toulouse   . . . This shit is amazing.

Saskia   This shit *is* amazing.

Toulouse   And you should take some coke.

Saskia   And I should take some coke.

Toulouse *hands her the tube with a tiny spoon and* **Saskia** *snorts a big bump from it.*

Saskia   Oh . . . Mother Teresa!

Toulouse   Cheers!

Fibre *tuts more loudly.*

Saskia   Sorry, what's up with her?

Toulouse   Oh, nothing, she's just on the spectrum –

Fibre   No, I just – I just wish I knew beforehand if I was, like, drinking with the literal embodiment of the devil.

Toulouse   Oh, Fibre, please –

Saskia   No, it's fine. You think I'm the devil?

Fibre   . . . It's not . . . you. It's just what you do?

Saskia   And what's that?

Fibre   . . . Developers. You come in here. You push all the poor people out. You put like . . . cameras and gyms, and . . . –

Saskia   Facilities?

Fibre   . . .

Saskia   What were you doing thirty years ago?

Fibre   Um, like, not existing?

Saskia   Well, neither did this area. My Aunt Paula lives just over there. See those flats. Used to come here all the time. Where do you lot shop?

Fibre   Tescos.

Toulouse   And the little Marks by the station –

Fibre *gives* **Toulouse** *a withering look.*

Saskia   Where do you eat?

Toulouse   Well, there's the Vietnamese, the Balkan place.

Saskia   And what do you do?

Fibre   I'm a communist.

Toulouse   . . . and a graphic designer.

Fibre (*to* **Toulouse**)   Shut up!

Saskia   Well, after you design all those graphics I'm sure you and your pals like a little boogie at the end of the week?

Fibre   Sometimes . . . –

Saskia *takes the tube of coke from* **Toulouse** *without asking and snorts again.*

Saskia   Well, when I came here to see my aunt, there was nothing. Eel pie and despair.

We brought the fun. Us *developers.*

Or, we made it safe so you could bring the fun. And your galleries and your vegan turnips –

Fibre   But –

Saskia   So, next time you open your mouth, you say a little prayer for the Pure Gyms, and the gates, and the cameras. OK? And the developers.

Toulouse   . . .

Saskia   Because we made this place.

Fibre   Maybe. But when does it all stop?

Saskia   Sorry?

Fibre   When does it all stop.

Saskia *is unable to answer.*

Saskia   . . .

Fibre   I think I want you to go.

Toulouse   No –

Fibre *exits and returns with her smart watch and hands it to* **Saskia***.*

Fibre   Yeah, you've put me well and truly in my place, so you can go now.

Toulouse (*to* **Fibre**)   Babe –

Fibre *closes the doors.*

Saskia *looks down at the watch in dismay.*

Saskia   But it's barely charged!

Fibre (*to* **Toulouse**)   Are you coming or not?

Toulouse   . . .

Fibre *tries to close the loft door behind them as* **Toulouse** *pokes his head out.*

Toulouse   DM me OK! I'm neonslut56 –

Fibre   Toulouse! –

Toulouse   All lower case –

Fibre *closes the loft door, and they both exit.*

Saskia *laughs and smiles as she, fuelled by the cocaine, walks down the canal.*

Saskia (*to audience, laughing*)   Bloody hippies,

hippy-crites,

they're all the same,

every time we make our claim.

Down in south, you know,

Aylesbury and Heygate, those old estates?

The Goldsmiths students, they squatted those, and refused
to go.

'We will not move! We are the people who live here!'

that was until the riot police came with their

shields and bats,

and they all slithered back to their sweet Dulwich flats.

Then the Spanish markets in Tottenham Hale,

'This is heart of the community! You are ripping the heart
out!'

They petitioned and protested,

and raised middle-class hell,

but in the end, they only ever ate at those markets once we
gutted them out.

'We shall not, we shall not be moved!'

Then the Tidemill Gardens,

in Deptford, south.

'We shall not be moved!'

That got a little Kumbaya.

Old ladies and shaggy punks,

chained up in the trees. And they wouldn't leave.

So in the dawn, we came in high-vis

and took out the trunks,

with a load of chainsaws.

She makes a beheading gesture with her finger against her neck and smiles as the sound.

And look, I don't like pulling old grannies from trees,

But in the end, as my horrible mother always said:

Money talks, and bullshit walks,

(*She points at audience.*)

And we're all part of the same beautiful mess,

cos as much as you lot love to moan,

you love your gyms and chai lattes,

just that little bit more.

She looks up at the canal. She stops, amazed.

. . . But . . .

no . . .

look,

My Aunt Paula's old flat!

She climbs through the fence of the canal to the council block of flats.

Same as it was,

deep grass growing by the deep canal,

me and Dizzy shuffled up,

and Paula welcomed us with open arms,

and ciggies,

and tea,

and a little whisky. And . . .

She gets round to her aunt's door.

It's dark and empty.

. . . But what's this . . .?

Saskia   Paula?

(To audience.) Flats all empty,

all boarded up. And broken in.

Saskia   Paula?

(To audience) 'Saskia!'

I can still hear Dizzy running through the hall.

She hears laughter.

She leaves the empty flat, spying the street through the window.

. . . Outside though,

there's the same old shops.

Chippy, laundrette . . . but all closed up. But there's the pub, that old punk place, where me and Dizzy snuck in one night and danced all . . . –

Now it's a bar for Rebellion Beer . . .

But . . . the corner shop! That's still there!

Mr . . . Rahman and free sweets and smiles and little paper bags!

But her face changes as she enters the shop.

But the shops all changed . . .

Posh courgettes and *Horse & Hound.*

Sammy *is price-tagging labels on things in the shop.*

He's young, good-looking, very affable.

Sammy   Hello!

Saskia *(to audience)*   Young man at the counter. Staring at me.

Saskia (*to* **Sammy**)   Hello. Do you know . . . Mr Rahman?

Sammy   Um . . . you mean my dad?

Saskia   Yeah. Yeah. I'm Saskia. Paula's niece?

Sammy   Oh, sure, Paula!

Saskia   What happened to the shops?

Sammy *keeps on price-tagging items as* **Saskia** *becomes agitated.*

Sammy   Most of them got bought out. We own it, so we stayed. See you just got to adapt. Making a killing now. You call a dog turd organic and they'll buy it –

Saskia   Who did it?

Sammy   Eckerd and Wise, Morley Estates, there was a couple of them –

Saskia   What happened to the flats?

Sammy   . . . Well, they all got moved on. They tear them down, then –

Saskia   Where did Paula go?!

Sammy   . . . I don't know. Essex?

She wouldn't go, they had to kick her out dragging and screaming.

Saskia*'s breathing gets worse.*

Sammy   . . . Aren't you her niece?

Saskia   I . . . –

Sammy. . . You OK?

Here, have an artichoke. Free of charge.

Saskia *has a panic attack. She falls into the stacks of shelves behind her, breaking things.*

Sammy   Oi, easy!

Saskia *staggers out of the shop, not able to breathe.*

Sammy *shouts after her.*

Sammy   Oi, you gonna pay for that?!

But **Saskia** *staggers back to the canal and vomits in the water.*

She then sits on the concrete behind her and lies back on it.

She hears singing, as someone plays a guitar lightly on the canal in her memory.

There is buzzing too.

Saskia (*to audience*)   . . . I remember my first panic attack.

It was right here. When this wasn't a building site.

It was trees, and grass, and little yellow flowers everywhere.

And me and Dizzy lay back here, all happily spliffed up as someone sang on the river bank.

I showed her the stories I'd written. I'd never shown anyone, except for Dad.

'These are good, Sask. Really good.'

She said, as I let my hand fall back in the grass, and picked one of those yellow flowers up.

But it wasn't a flower. 'Urgh!' It was a bee. A dead bee.

There were dead bees, everywhere.

'They come out cos they think it's summer'

said Dizzy, picking one up and twiddling it her hand. 'Cos it's so hot. And then they all die in the night.'

I started to pant.

'Once the bees have gone. We'll be gone too. Mum said the world will be under water in thirty years.'

'But that's fine.' She smiles. 'Thirty years is too long for me.'

'What do you mean, Diz . . .? What do you mean?'

But, as a I struggled to breathe, she took my hand, and smiled.

'Don't worry, Sask, we're here now.'

. . .

Her phone rings and merges with the buzzing. She finally picks it up. **Fraser** *sniffs a little and talks excitedly.* **Saskia**, *post-panic attack, is empty and mechanical.*

She answers her smart watch.

Fraser   . . . Saskia? Saskia? It's Fraser.

Saskia (*flatly*)   Yes.

Fraser   Listen, it's all good, you were right: the Union Collective, the community group. They signed the deal. It's all going through. We just need your signature and it's all good.

Saskia   Amazing.

Fraser   I know! We're done, Saskia, we've won.

Saskia   . . .

Fraser   And look – you know all the marshes, outside yours. Below Hackney Marshes.

Saskia   . . . What?

Fraser   I'm looking at it now. Who owns it?

Saskia   No, Fraser, it's just wasteland –

Fraser   Not if you drained it. Could be flats, patios, a pool –

Saskia   Fraser, no –

Fraser   I'll put in some calls. See you later, babe.

He ends the call. **Saskia** *slowly stands and walks to the water of the canal.*

Saskia (*to audience*)   I never wanted this deal, in Park Royal.

The mayor's office was meant to have it,

they were gonna build council homes, and proper flats,

and parks, and trees,

and the canal sweeping through. But they overstretched, fucked it up,

ran out of money. And lost the bid,

and every agent and prick with half a business degree,

went slobbering to the west. And Eckerd and Wise, they took the lot.

and I went round the shops,

and the churches,

and the streets. To their tenancy group: the Union Collective.

The same old bunch of single mums, stall-owners, knackered priests. To peddle the same old deal.

(*She makes ironic gesture with fingers.*) 40 per cent affordable.

A few council, to mix it up. And a little arts centre, that you'll never use,

and those figures, anyway, we will skew.

To keep you all out,

at the end of the day.

And now he even wants the marsh . . . where Dizzy, she . . . –

. . . Look at the water.

All black and deep.

She looks down at the canal and the water.

She allows her foot to hover above it.

She does not notice a light flicker on in a nearby canal boat, a door open and a woman holding a basin of dirty water.

I really can't swim.

Could just slip away . . .

Yeah, just slip, slip, slip away . . .

She is about to jump into the water.

But she is stopped, as the woman with the basin chucks the dirty water right into **Saskia***'s face.*

Lottie *is in her early thirties. Her hair is matted and she has a thick, colourful jumper on. She's kind.*

Lottie   Oh my God, I am so sorry –

Saskia   WHAT. IS. THIS.

Lottie   It's just aubergine bake.

Saskia   Oh God.

Lottie   Do you want a towel?

Saskia   Yes!

Lottie   Do you want some wine?

Saskia   YES!

Lottie *darts back inside her boat and then returns with a towel and a glass of wine which she hands to* **Saskia***.*

Lottie   I'm sorry, but – what were you doing, standing there?

Saskia   I was trying to kill myself.

Lottie (*laughs drily*)   Right.

There is crying from inside **Lottie***'s boat.*

Sorry.

She darts back inside the boat and returns holding a baby, wrapped up in a sheet. **Saskia** *melts.*

Saskia   Aw, look, a little boat baby.

Lottie   Yeah. Say hello, Karl.

Saskia   He's so cute.

Lottie   You got kids?

Saskia   Yeah, but not as cute as Karl. My kid looks like Bob Hoskins.

Lottie   No!

Saskia   Yes, but I love her to bits. Did you have her on the boat?

Lottie   Yeah, in a field actually.

Saskia   And do you two still have sex?

Lottie   . . . Er –

Saskia   I bet you do, don't you. I bet you have really sweaty carnal river sex and it's all musty and great.

Lottie   Um –

Saskia   Listen, you don't just want to . . . give me your life, do you? You can have mine. I've got central heating.

Lottie   Look, it's not that perfect. We . . . – I mean you have to shit in a box.

Saskia   What I'd do to shit in a box. Rocking gently on the water. Trees. Away from all this hell . . .

Lottie   I still love London. We come back as much as we can. It's still got that spirit. But . . .

Saskia   It's dying? . . .

Lottie   Maybe.

Saskia   But what can you do?

Lottie   I don't know . . . but but imagine we did nothing.
What would it look like then?

Saskia   . . .

The baby gurgles excitedly.

Lottie   Oh no, he'll never sleep now.

Saskia   When Rosa was really small. I'd put her to bed and
sit on the stair and drink wine and listen to her fall asleep.
Then I'd fall asleep.

Then I'd dream about her. We're doing this big
development, in the west. We're building this grand
restaurant. And I kept on dreaming about it. Me and Rosa,
sitting there, her a bit older, in a little dress. Eating with me.

And then the walls start to bleed. Not blood though, water.
Everything drips, and the room quickly fills up. But the
doors are locked. No one can get out. And then out the
window the whole city is drowning, it's drowning . . .

She buries her head in her hands, trying not to cry.

God, what is wrong with me! I used to be a people's person!

Lottie   Just tell me what's wrong.

Saskia   Everything! This person, this person you see
before: this is a machine. Something I've made. And it
doesn't work anymore.

Lottie   Since when?

Saskia   Since the deal, the fucking deal. That development,
we're just drowning the world in *shit*!

And now. Now Fraser even wants the marshes.

Lottie   So change things?

Saskia   Change things?

Lottie   About . . . your job, this deal.

Saskia   It's not just the job, it's me. It's wrapped up in one horrible mess and I can't do anything now to change it. It's too late . . .

She buries her head.

Lottie   Look, why don't I call someone? Pick you up.

Saskia   No, I have to finish this. I have to run home.

Lottie   Why?

Saskia   Because we never finished it. We never went home. There was this . . . party on Hackney Marshes. With all the cool kids, Shanice Lane, Melissa.

Lottie   . . .

Saskia   I never wanted to go, I told her!

Lottie   . . . What happened to her? Your friend . . .?

Saskia   She died. She died because of me.

Lottie   . . .

Saskia *stands up and wipes her face, smiling.*

Saskia   Listen, thank you for the wine. And the baby. And your life is great, well done –

Lottie   Wait –

Saskia   But I need to go. I've got calls to make –

Lottie   Wait.

She puts the baby down and then wraps the thin towel around **Saskia***'s leg, to support her bruised ankle.*

Lottie   Listen . . . I don't know you. I don't know anything about you but . . .

you finish your run. If it's important to you, you finish it.

And listen: you can always change things. If you really want to, you can change it. Just find what makes you happy.

Write your own story.

Saskia   . . . Thank you.

Lottie   And be careful: it's going to rain.

Although she hobbles,

Saskia *starts to run. She has regained her former composure. Along the towpath, kicking up dust.*

Saskia (*to audience*)   . . . find what makes me happy . . . yeah . . . write my own story . . .

Path all dark and dusty. Bats and birds screech through the air.

Come on, Saskia. Remember Brighton,

that run in Fife.

The half-marathon you did in Bournemouth where you nearly did a Paula Radcliffe in your pants but you didn't:

you didn't do a Paula in your pants because you are Saskia Dunne!

Queen of the 10k run!

Plus you eat a hell of a lot of fibre.

There is a glow of street-lamp.

. . . But wait . . .

I know this place . . . Victoria Park.

There's the fountain. The little loos.

That's where Rosa did a massive poo.

Ice-cream shack, bit for prams.

Oh my God:

it's MUMMY LAND!

Oh, sweet dog bowls,

and yoga mats . . .

And yes, there, Stratford rising up in the east! I'm home.

But then the path splits in two . . .

One home, to Stratford. And the other, to where I was born
. . .

to Bromley and Bow. The route me and Dizzy took, all those years ago . . .

American Sarah   Saskia?

Saskia (*to audience*)   Light feet padding up,

Someone calls my name . . .

American Sarah   Saskia, is that you?

Saskia (*to audience*)   It's American Sarah, one of the yoga mums. Oh, I hug her like a hot-cross bun!

American Sarah, *a local mum from the gated community that* **Saskia** *lives in, jogs up and recognises* **Saskia**. *She is tall, slim and athletic.*

Saskia *is elated to see her and takes* **American Sarah**'*s hands and hugs her.*

Saskia   Oh my God, American Sarah!

(*To audience.*) She recoils –

American Sarah   Saskia, what's that on you? What's that on you?

Saskia   It's aubergine. Where have you been?

American Sarah   At our book club.

Saskia   What are you reading?

American Sarah   *Normal People*. Have you read it?

Saskia   No, but I want to.

Saskia *takes her hand.*

Listen, Sazza. Can I call you Sazza?

American Sarah   No –

Saskia   Listen, Sazza, I don't know what happened tonight on the canal, but . . . I want to change things. I want to be your friend. I want . . . to go the farmers' market with you. I want to observe kale. I want to sell cakes and raise money for blind dolphins or some crazy shit!

American Sarah   But, Saskia, you never liked that stuff –

Saskia   I know! But I'm changed –

American Sarah   And you never liked me. Or any of us.

Saskia   . . .

American Sarah   See, I was gonna go to your party tonight but Leon turned me away. Something about . . . *asbestos*?

Saskia   . . .

Listen, Sarah.

See, the old me, she would have lied. She would have made up some elaborate lie about asbestos being in some unknown cupboard and got everyone else to lie about it to your face. All while serving cake.

But that's the old me.

Because it's true: I didn't like you, Sarah. I found you annoying, and basic. And for some reason you smell a bit like yeast.

But it's because I didn't appreciate you. I didn't appreciate this life we've got.

American Sarah   . . . Right.

Saskia   But I do now. I do.

American Sarah   . . .

Saskia   So what's say we saddle up, and head home in time for cake and bubbles.

American Sarah *runs away.* **Saskia** *calls after.*

Saskia   Wait, Sarah.

American Sarah!

American Sarah *stops.*

American Sarah   I'm not American, bitch! I'm Canadian. You just never asked.

Saskia   . . .

American Sarah   Listen, Saskia, I may be annoying, I may smell of yeast. But at least I know it.

Saskia   Sarah –

American Sarah   And at least I'm not insane.

Saskia   . . .

American Sarah   Oh, yeah. Lydia saw you out on the marshes. Talking to yourself. Knee-deep in the water.

Saskia   No . . .

American Sarah   Who were you talking to?

Saskia   No . . .

Now **Saskia** *runs away.*

American Sarah   We all know *you*, Saskia, you just don't know yourself!

Saskia   No!

She runs away from her, the other direction.

She turns to audience, all smiles again.

A beautiful hymn is heard.

Saskia (*to audience*)   No worries, American Sarah goes her way . . .

I go mine,

to my real home, to Bromley and Bow. That's the way we took anyway . . . and I'll skirt back up to Stratford in time for tea and cake.

Yes there, look!

At Mile End Park,

lovers entwined droop down and sip last tinnies in the dusk,

Down in Limehouse,

by the bridge, basin full of rocking boats.

I had my first kiss. Chris Hutton, by blue-flecked light and glinting syringe.

'You know what, Sask,' he said, parting my hair,

'You're not as ugly as I thought, you know.'

'Cheers' but then he took me up the hill,

and with golden city burning on the fringe,

the cool kids partied and drank fake champagne:

'Oh, Sask, you're alright you know,' said Shanice Lane. Shanice Lane!

'We're having a party on the marshes next week, you should come!'

Me! The marshes!

'Yeah, but,' Melissa Brown barked up, 'I swear you're friends with that Dizzy?'

'That one with her dad in Hackney nut house.'

Shanice froze, Melissa laughed:

'She done you by the chicken shop, Shanice!' Shanice turned to me:

'Is that true, are you friends with that lesbian?'

'No!' I laughed back, still swaying to garage played on phones. 'No, of course not.'

'Good.' Shanice smiled. 'Cos I'm gonna fuck her up.'

The gospel singing gets louder as singers emerge from a church. **Saskia** *looks and smiles.*

. . . And just as I reminisce

from the old, tin maritime, by the pub, the Star of the East,

three ladies wrapped in cloth shuffle out,

praising Jesus and thrusting hands to the night sky and singing the most beautiful song I have ever heard.

She moves to the music.

But then, from gated, penthouse flats –

'Excuse me.'

Some beetroot-faced man shoots out his flap and bellows quietly at us:

'We're trying to eat polenta in here. This is actually a quiet zone after 8.45p.m. . . .'

. . . and we fall back, deflated . . .

. . . .But then . . .

one of the robed ladies shoots back up:

'So shut the fuck up then!'

and beetroot man, startled,

'Oh God!'

turtles back behind his flap.

And we all resume.

we all stand,

we all sing,

down there, by the Star of the East.

Saskia *dances slowly to the beautiful hymn, humming to herself, by the bridge.*

She does not notice **Dev***, female, and* **Kade***, male, watch her. They are both in their twenties, both gaunt and their clothes dishevelled, both drug-addicts.*

Saskia (*to audience*)   . . . but what I don't see,

is two crackheads by the bridge,

abusing some poor Lime Bike,

slap it down and turn their gaze on me . . .

The music slowly drifts away as her smart watch rings again.

She finally notices it and answers the phone call in a daze. It's **Fraser***.*

Fraser   Saskia.

Saskia   Fraser . . .

Fraser   We need to talk about the deal.

Saskia   Yes . . . yes we do –

Fraser   We can't build the park. And the council houses . . . – we just can't afford it.

Saskia   But . . . we've signed. We can't get out of that –

Fraser   Well . . . not if we grease a few palms at the Housing Office. I know a guy . . .

Saskia   . . . But that's illegal –

Fraser   That's life. We just can't afford it. And if we don't get the bid tonight it will go back to the Mayor's office and they'll just fuck it up.

Saskia   . . .

Fraser   . . . Saskia, I was gonna offer you partner tonight.

Saskia   . . .

Fraser   Yeah, that's right: Eckerd, Wise and Dunne: the fastest-growing property firm in Western Europe. Do you want that?

Saskia   . . . of course.

Fraser   So get home now. Also, that swamp outside yours? I put in some calls. It's wide open, I mean there's some local types hanging about –

Saskia   . . . is Leon there?

Fraser   . . . Sure. I'll get that little wet bag

Saskia   Don't call him that –

Fraser (*calling off*)   Leon!

. . .

Saskia *stiffens up. She sees* **Dev** *and* **Kade** *watching her.*

Saskia (*to audience*)   But then, at the bridge, I see their eyes. Mean, and hungry, and scag-head high –

Leon *answers the phone.*

Leon   Saskia?

Saskia   Leon . . . Leon – listen, watch Fraser –

Leon   What?

Saskia   Whatever he asks you to do, don't do it, wait for me. And, and –

Leon   Saskia –

Saskia   Whatever happens. Just remember. That I love you. If there's one thing I know, I love you.

Leon   . . .

But that's not what you said last night –

Saskia   I meant that . . . I'm not in love with what *you've* become. What *I've* become! This fucking life. Our flat from a catalogue. All the cheese-plants –

Leon   You bought the cheese-plants!

Saskia   I know. But I don't want them anymore. I don't want any of it . . . –

. . . When I was young . . . I thought my life would have more . . . colour. Me and Dizzy . . . we used to dream, and dream and dream.

Leon   . . . What happened to her, Sask?

What happened on the marsh?

Saskia *turns to* **Dev** *and* **Kade**, *who move closer.*

Leon   Listen, Sask. Remember when we met. At the office party.

Saskia   . . . I was a mess.

Leon   And you talked to me. Little office dweeb. Graphic designer –

Saskia   I liked your eyes.

Leon   . . . and remember we just left. We just left and walked, walked back all the way here through the city. And just talked. And talked. About everything. About books. About . . . what we wanted to do. Our dreams.

Saskia   I showed you my writing, when we got back to mine. I'd never showed anyone.

Leon   I couldn't believe those stories. That someone like you, someone so perfect, could have that weird, beautiful, world in their head.

Saskia   . . . You were the first person I could ever talk to. Well, the second . . .

Leon   So talk to me. What happened to her?

Saskia   . . .

Leon   Cos whatever it is, you gotta let it in.

Saskia   . . .

(*To audience.*) The Crackies close in!

(*She sees something.*) Wait, Leon, wait!

Suddenly, **Dev** *and* **Kade** *rush in and grab* **Saskia***, to mug her.* **Saskia** *resists them as best she can.* **Saskia** *can describe this or they can physically rush her.*

The wolves tear and bite –

Saskia   Fuck off, no –!

They struggle together.

Saskia (*to audience*)   They push me down. Leon screaming on the end of the phone!

Dev   Get her bag, bruv!

Kade   I can't!

Dev *tuts and then kicks* **Saskia** *hard in the stomach.* **Saskia** *keels over and falls to the ground.*

She whimpers on the ground as **Dev** *takes her belt bag with her credit cards.*

A police siren flashes and wails close by, **Dev** *looks to it fearfully.*

Kade *tries to take* **Saskia***'s smart watch but* **Saskia** *holds it tight against her body.*

Saskia   Leave her alone. Please leave her alone.

Kade   Leave who alone?

Saskia   Dizzy, leave her alone.

Dev   Take the watch, man!

Kade   I don't think she's alright, you know.

Dev   Who cares, take the watch!

A police siren wails again, louder, closer, flashing blue and red across the scene. **Dev***, startled, runs away.*

Dev   Fuck, feds, just go, just go!

Dev *exits.*

Saskia   Please, no . . . leave her alone . . .

Kade *watches* **Saskia** *mutter to herself.*

Kade   . . . I'm sorry.

Kade *slowly exits.*

Saskia *is left alone, shaking on the floor.*

In the distance, thunder can be heard growling.

She starts to crawl along the floor.

Light, sad string music plays like Michael Nyman's 'The Other Side'.

Saskia (*to audience*)   I crawl along a bit,

through piss and puddles,

Factories loom up and down and blue light drips,

Me and Dizzy sat here that day, against the sun,

(*Sunlight enters as she remembers* **Dizzy**.)

now moon.

We were out of weed. We were nearly home . . .

to Stratford . . .

to Dizzy's mad, lovely mum, and tea, and conspiracies,

and shit homemade scones and stories of her dad who died.
Who drowned.

She handed me the last of the spliff.

And saw the bruises on my arm . . .

'Was that your mum?' she asked as I covered them in sleeve.

'No'

Dizzy looked down,

'She's a cow.'

'Don't call her that!'

'Why?'

'Because you don't call your mum that.'

She sprang up.

'But she is, she won't even let you write, she won't let even
let you go uni!'

'Cos she needs me' I snapped back. On the concrete steps,

'She's alone, she's getting sick, she needs me to work. She
needs me.'

. . . It's so easy for you, everything's so easy. You never had
to choose, you never had to struggle . . .'

But then . . . the sun glints on her arm.

And I see the slash marks, coiling up, like barbed wire, made
with a knife.

'And anyway,' I hiss back, 'I never ask about them scratches
on your arm.'

She smiled weakly.

'You could. If you wanted . . .'

But I didn't . . .

. . . then she jumped up suddenly and squealed,

'I know!'

but Dizzy, she had another idea.

'Let's go to the party on the marsh!' she wailed and pointed east.

'No!'

But off she ran . . .

'Dizzy, no!'

Sunlight disappears. Now moonlight.

Kerry   Hello?

Saskia (*to audience*)   But then . . . another voice . . .

by the bridge, against the moon . . .

an old lady with bags shuffles down . . .

. . .

Kerry *enters.*

She is an older woman in her sixties, with a cockney accent, wearing a white coat and carrying two large bags from the nearby supermarket, Lidl.

She is startled to see **Saskia** *lying on the floor, whimpering.*

Kerry   You alright, there? Hello?

You really shouldn't lie there, you know.

There's dog shit down there. And glass.

And dead cats.

I once saw a cat die right where your head is now.

Saskia   . . .

Kerry   Are you OK?

Saskia   . . .

Kerry   Alright, budge up. And close your legs dear, have some dignity.

So, what happened to you?

Saskia   . . . I got mugged.

Kerry   Oh dear.

Saskia   They're scum.

Kerry   And bored.

Saskia *tries to leave but her foot is badly sprained.*

Kerry   Where you goin'?

Saskia   I need to make some calls.

She tries to call using her smart watch but it doesn't work.

Saskia   Fuck – do you have a charger for a Smart-Watch X?

Kerry   . . .?

Saskia   Fuck.

Kerry   Look, chill your fanny for a bit. And have a Belgian bun. They were reduced.

She rummages in her bag and takes out a plastic container with buns in it.

Kerry   You from around here, then?

Saskia   . . . I was.

. . . used to live on Brewer Street.

Kerry   Oh yeah, posh.

Saskia   Wasn't then.

Kerry   I live on Canning Estates.

Saskia   . . . they tore those down.

Kerry   They can't get the last of them, not with us still in 'em.

The developers they offered us a place in Ilford. Now who do I know in Ilford?

Saskia   Us?

Kerry   . . . Sorry, me . . . Paul . . . my husband. He died.

Saskia   . . . I'm sorry.

Kerry   Don't be. At my age everyone dies. Or moves to Ilford. Which is basically the same thing.

Saskia *laughs just a little.*

Kerry   All I've got is memories. I walk around and swim in them. See, over there, those posh flats? That was my school. And see that little restaurant. That used to be a pub. I got nicely shagged there in the car park.

Saskia (*laughing slightly*)   No.

Kerry   Oh, yeah, I was quite the little thing! I got shagged all up and down this borough.

Saskia *laughs.* **Kerry** *rummages in her bag and takes out a tiny bottle of wine.*

Kerry   Have a tiny bottle of wine.

Saskia   . . . Nah, I can't.

Kerry   Go on, it's Friday, have a tiny bottle of wine.

Saskia *takes and drinks the wine.*

Saskia   This *is* a tiny bottle of wine.

Kerry   Yeah, saves me from becoming an alcoholic. Although I'm trying to get into weed. Do you know anyone who could get me some weed?

Saskia   So you liked it better back then? When you were young.

Kerry Well, maybe it was more rough, back in my day. But we looked out for each other. And there were jobs. And the pubs were always full.

That's what I'll never get used to, when they clean a place up: the silence. It's so silent.

Saskia So you never went to Ilford?

Kerry No, but they tried. First they send the nice lady round from the developers. She's all smiles. 'Ilford's very lovely, if you give it a try.' I got rid of her sharpish.

Saskia How?

Kerry Came on to her! Made her a big curry and touched her leg. She left double-quick.

Saskia *laughs.*

Kerry Then they send some man from Tower Hamlets round. He's not so nice.

'Mrs Galloway, you have to take the deal. You'll be living on a bombsite otherwise!'

Well, I tell 'em I was born on a bombsite, I'll die on one.

Saskia How'd you get rid of him?

Kerry Cup of piss in the face. Cockney old school. Classic.

Saskia Nice.

Kerry But then it turns nasty. They cut the gas. Then the water.

Saskia . . . What?

Kerry Oh, yeah. See once your place is marked for demolition the council have no obligation anymore. They let it rot. With you still inside.

Saskia No –

Kerry   I'm telling you, yes! And it weren't just me. My friends, my family, the ones that stayed. My mate, they dragged him out at dawn by his teeth, a man of eighty-three. Cos he wouldn't leave.

Saskia   No –

Kerry   Then you go online. My sister showed me. These forums. It's not just here. It's everywhere. They're privatising Ridley Road market. Build a car park on Mudchute Farm. Turn Peckham into a shopping mall –

Saskia   No –

Kerry   And now they want to build this whole new city out west! In Park Royal. I swear to God, it's a conspiracy. And it's not just London. My mate showed me. It's other cities too. It's Paris, it's San Frisco, Berlin, Lisbon, Seoul, Johannesburg. It's feckin' everywhere. I swear, they won't stop until the world's one big fucking . . . Pret!

Saskia   No, it's not like that!

Kerry   What you talking about? You don't know!

Saskia   I do.

Kerry   How?

Saskia   Because . . . I'm a developer, OK? And I'm sorry . . . you feel that way. But we don't do it like that.

Kerry   . . .

Saskia   I'm not saying it's perfect. But it's progress.

Kerry   I've seen you –

Saskia   Not everyone wins but . . .

Kerry   At one of those meetings –

Saskia   It's just the way it is. It's change. It's . . . inevitable.

She stands, painfully.

Kerry   . . . No, it ain't. Cos us lot we got together. And we found other groups. Community groups. And we got all together and we went down to Ridley Road Market, and Mudchute, and Peckham, and we screamed and shouted long enough that you lot, you lot didn't win, even with those crooked councillors.

Saskia *tries to leave.*

Kerry   See? It works. If you get together, it works. Yeah, change is inevitable.

But what you lot do, your . . . *violence*, that's not.

Saskia   That's rubbish. It's just . . . business. We don't hurt people.

Kerry   You hurt my husband.

Saskia   . . .

Kerry   The damp in the walls battered his lungs. And when the ambulance come, they couldn't get up the stairs cos it was all smashed up. He died in that room.

You lot did that. I don't care what you say.

You killed him.

Saskia *hobbles away.*

Kerry   And we're watching you, you know.

That city in Park Royal, we'll be there.

And the north, and the south, and the east, and the west.

We'll be there, to protect what's left.

The sky above rumbles.

There's a storm coming, Saskia, there's a storm.

Saskia *hobbles away, her ankle damaged.* **Kerry** *exits.*

Saskia *turns to audience.*

Saskia (*to audience*)   Come on, Saskia. Got to make the call.
You know the place.

She hits a horseshoe and screams in pain, picking it up, incredulous.

Fuck! A horseshoe?!

What is this: Steptoe-and-fucking-cunt!

*She hurls the horseshoe across the ground and screams at the
audience.*

See!

This is what happens when you don't have properly
franchised coffee shops.

You get horseshoes,

You get abused by Lidl witches.

I swear this must be the last like it.

The last place where the cranes didn't get.

Where we didn't slap out signs. Eckerd and Wise.

But God as my witness, when we're done with the west,

we shall come back here and fill it in!

She stops moving as something glows white on the canal.

Something flashes white and she hears a bird call.

But then, from some tiny bit of tree,

from some factory.

… it can't be. That bird again. Impossible.

But yes. Same black streaks.

'Dizzy . . .'

And she looks at me. And then lifts her wings. And flies east
. . .

But she turns away, frowning, leaving the canal and going through some rusted gates, down residential streets.

But no . . .

gotta make the call.

Slip through grim familiar streets, less grim now to . . .

. . . there it is.

My old high street . . . haven't been in years.

All nice and cleaned up.

Gone are the Ladbrokes. The mean old drunks.

The kids who spit and snarl and spunk their lives up the wall.

And there's our pub. Formerly the Rose.

I got fingered over by those bins. Chris Hutton again:

'You like that, babe.'

'Oh, yeah.'

Oh no, he was shit. But it was Chris Hutton. What could I say?

Then he sat me down for a post-finger chat:

'Hey, Sask. Why do you always hang out with Dizzy, that freak?'

'. . . I don't, Chris.'

I lied.

'You've got that all wrong.'

. . .

Bells ring of a pub door being opened. **Saskia** *sits at stool.* **Hip Ed** *is at the counter, drying a glass. He's a trendy young man in his twenties with a big moustache. He has a faint Australian accent.*

The Rose is now the Tap and inside it's all stainless steel and wasabi nuts.

Hip Ed   Hiya, what can I get you

The moustached man asks at the counter, caressing a menu:

Saskia   A pint of wine please.

Hip Ed *laughs hysterically. Saskia does not. He stops laughing.*

Hip Ed   … I can do a large glass.

Saskia   Great. Do you have a charger for a Smart-Watch 5?

Hip Ed (*squealing with pleasure*)   Of course!

Hip Ed *takes* **Saskia***'s smart watch and connects it to a charger. He then takes a large glass out and pours wine into from an orange bottle.*

Hip Ed   Rough night.

Saskia   You have no idea.

He finishes pouring but it's a tiny amount.

Hip Ed   That will be £16 please.

Saskia *frowns.*

Hip Ed   It's orange.

Saskia *sighs and then goes for her credit-card in her belt bag.* **Hip Ed** *holds a card machine. But then she remembers:*

Saskia   Oh fuck.

Hip Ed   Everything cool?

Saskia   Um, look mate… I got mugged, and.

Hip Ed   …

Saskia   But listen, I live just up there. In Lea Mansions.

Hip Ed *takes back the glass.*

Hip Ed   I'm sorry, we don't really do that.

Saskia *grabs the glass too.*

Saskia   Look, mate, I've had a fucking rough night –

Hip Ed   I understand.

Saskia   No, you don't understand. You don't understand a fucking thing, you moustacheo-ed prick!

Saskia (*to audience*)   The glass swirls between us, threatening to explode,

Chris Hutton *enters.*

Chris   Saskia?

Saskia (*to audience*)   . . . but then a voice, a voice . . .

Saskia *turns around and is amazed.*

Chris   Saskia, is that you?

Saskia (*to audience*)   Behind me, as if appearing from a dream . . .

Saskia   Chris.

Chris *is in his mid-thirties.*

Still good-looking but a little chubbier.

His t-shirt is a little stained with mud.

Chris   Saskia.

Saskia *hugs him, tightly.*

Chris   Woah.

Saskia (*to audience*)   Moustache man still quivers there with his card machine.

Chris   I'll get this.

Saskia (*to audience*)   But Chris taps him out and he scurries away.

Chris   a little balder, a little fatter but . . . –

They sit down and smile, drinking their drinks.

Chris   . . . Saskia Dunne. You look amazing.

Saskia   No . . . do I?

Chris   But is that aubergine? –

Saskia   Do I? Do I really look amazing?

Chris   . . . Yeah! I mean . . . you were such a mess before.

Saskia   Cheers –

Chris   Like braces, and frizzy hair, it was a little monstrous –

Saskia   OK, cheers –

Chris   I'm joking. I liked you.

They smile.

Chris   . . . You married?

Saskia   Yes, but you knew that. You?

Chris   Yep. And you knew that?

Saskia   Mum.

Chris   Oh yeah, how is she? Did she . . . get better?

Saskia   Yes, unfortunately.

Chris   . . .

Saskia   You happy in your marriage?

Chris   . . . Yeah, I'd say . . . – about 60 per cent happy?

Saskia   And you're a gardener, right?

Chris   Yeah, landscaping.

It's mostly with with schools, local kids, charities. We build play-parks. Little allotments.

Saskia   . . . Wow.

Chris   Yeah, we're trying to do a big thing up on the marshes. Build a wetland centre. Canoeing for the kids. Maybe an open-air theatre.

Saskia   Amazing.

Chris (*smiling*)   Yeah, that is if you lot don't get there first.

Saskia   . . . So you heard about that.

Chris   I'm kidding –

She raises her glass.

Saskia   Wow. Chris. Man of the people.

And me: Saskia Dunne. Gentrifying scum.

Chris   . . . I didn't say that.

Saskia   But you think it.

Saskia   . . .

Chris   I just can't believe it, Sask. A developer, I mean . . . I always thought you'd be like an artist or actor or –

Saskia   Yeah, well, I always thought you'd be a prick.

He takes her hand.

Chris   . . . I'm sorry. I always really liked you. And her. I guess I always thought I had to be a prick. I guess I was waiting . . . to be someone better.

Saskia   And I was waiting to be someone worse . . .

She lowers her head in her hands and tries not to cry.

Chris   . . . Saskia?

She takes his hand.

Saskia   Chris, listen.

It is better round here, isn't it?

Chris   . . .

Saskia   You know it was a dump. Shitty shops and getting mugged every time you went out.

Chris   I don't know –

Saskia   . . . But it is better, isn't it. Now? You have to say that, right?

Chris   . . . It's better. It's worse. It's good. It's bad.

Who knows. But I do know: the bad stuff, once that takes over. Takes hold of a bit of the city you love. You can't get it back.

Saskia   But what can we do?

Chris   Protect it. Hold on to what you love. Cos if decent people don't do decent things. Then the whole city is fucked. It's gone.

Saskia   . . .

. . .

You've changed. Very different fingers from the boy who fingered me by the bins.

Chris *laughs.*

Chris   . . . You've changed too.

Saskia *buries her head in her hands and cries. He takes her hands to comfort her.*

Chris   Sask, what's wrong?

Saskia   I'm . . . I'm about to do something terrible. Worse . . . worse than what I've done before.

Chris   I'm sure . . . you can get out of it.

Saskia   I can't. It's too big now. It's too big.

But maybe I can do one thing. One good thing.

Chris   . . .?

Saskia   See that bit of Hackney Marshes, the one you want for the centre?

Chris   Yeah?

Saskia   . . . My boss wants it. But if you get on it now, if you get the community together, if you make some calls.

Chris   Is he serious?

Saskia   Yeah, he'll have them writing the contracts, twisting councillors' arms. And, listen: once he gets going, there's nothing you can do to stop him.

Chris   . . . Alright. I know who to call.

Saskia   Really?

Chris   Yeah, we got a decent residents' association here. And there's a few good councillors left at Tower Hamlets.

He gets up from his stool.

. . . The marshes, yeah?

Saskia   Yeah.

Chris   . . . That's where it happened, innit. With Dizzy.

Saskia   . . .

Chris   I can't believe that . . . the way they found her. I mean . . . did she reach out to you? Did she call?

Saskia *stands and turns to audience.*

Saskia (*to audience*)   . . . the room spins.

Chris   What happened to you two? You were so tight. What happened that day?

Saskia (*to audience*)   It spins again. I screech my stool back.

Chris   Where you goin'?

Saskia (*to audience*)   And lean over and get my watch.

Chris   Saskia, where you goin'?!

Sound of thunder and the street outside. Lights of street.

Saskia (*to audience*)   And out into the sweaty street,

with sky fat and rumbling and angry.

Chris   SASKIA! WAIT!

Saskia (*to audience*)   And through High Road,

past more wasabi pubs, and tapas joints,

where new mums and dads lament the price of eggs.

'Eggs have gone wild!'

. . . and then my little street.

Ex-council. Stainless-steeled and gutted.

white stone gardens and posh palms,

doorbells with cameras

. . . and there's that little park. Where me and Dizzy fought hydras and ghouls,

But next to that . . .

the last shabby door on that last shabby bit of street.

. . . I ring.

She rings a doorbell.

Mum *answers. She wears a nightie and looks exhausted.*

Her face was once pretty but has been ravaged by a life of worry and anger. Slight cockney accent.

Saskia (*to audience*)   . . . and a woman pops out in a night-gown, and scowls.

Saskia   . . . Hiya, Mum.

Mum   Saskia . . .?

Saskia (*to audience*)   She can't believe her sunken eyes.

Saskia   You don't happen to a have charger for a Smart-Watch 5, do you?

Mum   You're drunk.

Saskia   Actually, I think it's alright, think I got some charge.

Mum   . . . please don't come here if you're drunk.

Saskia   Never stopped you.

Mum   . . .

Saskia   I heard you let Jesus into your life. What's he like?

Mum   I heard you let money into yours. And corruption and greed.

Saskia   I thought you liked money.

Mum   . . . Yeah, enough to put food on the table. To give you decent things when your mug of a dad . . . –

I only wanted to provide.

Saskia   You liar. You used to slap me around the face with my books: 'None of this matters, this reading,' you'd say, 'it's money that matters.'

Mum   Cos we had nothing! I wanted a decent life for us. Not those dreams and dumb ideas your dad planted before he fucked off for ever. I wanted you to succeed. But not this. Not ripping the heart of the place that made you.

Saskia   . . . I –

Mum   What?

Saskia   I did it for you.

Don't you understand? I did it so you would one day take me in your hands and say, 'Well done. Well done.'

I did it for that . . . that one moment. You made this, you made it . . .

Mum   . . .

Saskia   . . .

Mum   I'm sorry about Dizzy. I heard . . .

Saskia   . . .

Mum   . . .

Saskia   . . . Listen, Mum. Could you just . . . just for a bit . . .

Mum   . . .

Saskia   Could you hold me . . .?

Mum   . . .

Saskia   You don't have to mean it. But could you hold me
. . .?

Mum   . . . I –

Saskia (*to audience*)   . . . She holds the door.

She hesitates.

Mum   . . . Please don't come here when you're drunk.

Saskia (*to audience*)   And shuts it neatly in my face.

. . .

. . .

. . .

Saskia *stands there. Then thunder is heard above her. She hobbles
back along the high street, back to the canal.*

She calls her smart watch.

She turns to audience.

. . . it starts to rain.

. . . Light.

Then fat dusty drops of rain, of –

but I keep going,

back to the high street,

back on the canal, hobble through growling, prowling dark, where it splits into the River Lea,

and . . .

gravel path turns tarmac,

rubber runway running to the sky,

and Stratford. And the Olympic Bowl beneath.

Where I call.

Fraser *picks up on smart watch.*

Fraser   Saskia?! Saskia, where the fuck are you?

Saskia   I'm close. I want to sign the contract, now. How long we got?

Fraser   Half an hour.

Saskia   OK, meet me in the Wick, you know the Tank?

Fraser   Of course, we built it.

Saskia   Bring the contract.

She ends the call and hobbles along the path. A bird tweets in the distance.

Saskia (*to audience*)   . . . and there she is: the jewel in the crown:

Hackney Wick,

plastic pints and New York all night.

But then the road splits . . .

to the left, the Wick,

then the right . . .

. . . Hackney Marshes . . .

yellow fields of scrub and city wheat and willow trees dipping down go on for ever,

and something sparkles in the night.

Sunlight shimmers as she remembers.

'Come on!'

Dizzy and me, sat here at this split.

I sat, she stood.

'Come on! Let's go to the party!'

'No!'

'Why?!'

She turned to me, against burning sky.

'You're embarrassed by me, aren't you?'

I couldn't even lie.

'You're a fake, Saskia. You're a ghost.'

'And what are you? Billy-no-mates, the freak.'

'It's just so easy for you. You just let it all out!'

'And you never let it in!'

'And why should I?' I snarled, 'So I can end up like you? Like your dad? In the nut-house. Then . . .'

. . . She stopped again, and the trees waved behind . . .

'I'm sorry, Diz.'

but then, she simply replied,

'at least when he took his own life, Sask. He knew who he was.'

. . . before speeding off, up to the marsh.

'No!'

'One day Saskia' she turned back as she ran,

'You're gonna have to decide who you are!'

. . .

Saskia *stares ahead in disbelief. She hears a bird call.*

. . . but no

It can't be. There's that bird again. Looking at me . . .

before flying off, to the marsh, east . . .

She hesitates, about to turn right, towards the marshes . . .

. . . but in the end she turns left, to Hackney Wick.

She walks through the drunken revelries and many clubs of Hackney Wick with forced enthusiasm: the fairly unfriendly crowds make her nervous.

But no,

This time I turn away.

. . . up to the Wick,

to chicken wings and cocaine strips,

cos I know who I am: I'm Saskia Dunne: gentrifying scum. And that's all it is.

to the Tank. The coup de grace. Five storeys of blah, blah, blah.

Fraser   Saskia? . . . Saskia?!

Saskia (*to audience*)   As I slip past the angry bouncer,

who holds his nose, Fraser sits on a fake-wooden stool,

Fraser   Saskia! Over here!

*She sees **Fraser** and goes over to him excitedly but falls in the crowd. He helps her up.*

Fraser   Jesus Christ, are you alright?

Saskia   Oh, Fraser. Thank God.

Fraser   Take it easy.

Saskia   I'm just so happy, I'm just so happy to be home . . .

Fraser   Look, take a seat . . . do you want a pint?

Saskia   Yes.

She surveys the room happily.

(*To audience.*) He slips off and skips the queue,

we are the boss of this place and all . . .

and yes . . .

a balding man eats bowlfuls of cheesy chips,

. . . an absolutely pissed woman in PR gyrates by a cheese-plant,

this is home.

Fraser   There you go.

Saskia (*to audience*)   He returns with a frothy pint of IPA and chicken wings.

Fraser   Jesus!

Saskia (*to audience*)   He squeals as I devour the lot.

Fraser   What's happened to you?

Saskia   I got gang-banged by a city. Where's the contract?

Fraser   Here. It's on the screen.

He hands her an electronic tablet with the contract on its screen.
Saskia *scrolls through it.*

Fraser   What happened tonight, Saskia?

Saskia   . . .

Fraser   Don't lie. I won't be angry. Just tell me.

Saskia   OK, so I obviously . . . went a little bit mental.

Fraser   . . .

Saskia   OK, a big bit mental. But I'm honestly alright now. I just . . . I just had some things. That were a bit muddled in my head. But it's all gone now. I promise.

Fraser   But . . . what's that in your hair?

Saskia   It's aubergine. Some hippy threw it on me.

Fraser   Where's your stuff?

Saskia   Well, then I got mugged, then some Lidl hag tried to cast a spell on me. And there was a this white bird –

Fraser   Bird?

Saskia   Yes, it was fucking Greek to be honest.

Fraser   Greek?

Saskia   Yeah, but it's done now. I'm back in Ithaca. And I'm ready to shag and eat some bulls.

Fraser   . . .?

Saskia   I'm Odysseus? Done my trails and I'm home? You know, the *Odyssey*? Homer?

Fraser   . . .

Saskia   You really need to read more, Fraser.

Fraser   But it's done, yeah? Your head is clear?

Saskia   Definitely.

Fraser (*leaning back in chair*)   . . . So why do I get a call from the office saying that my bid for the marsh land has been blocked?

Saskia   . . .

Fraser   Blocked by local do-gooder, and your childhood sweetheart: Chris-the-man-Hutton?

Saskia   . . .

Fraser   Sask, listen: I don't care about that scrub-land, you want to save you old stomping ground, fine. You should have said.

I'm not a monster, Sask.

Saskia   . . . No.

Fraser   And anyway, I don't care about that swamp. I care about this deal. I care about you.

He takes her hand.

Saskia   . . . How's the party?

Fraser   Anaemic. Some guys from HR tried to start a conga and Leon nearly wet his pants.

Saskia *laughs.*

Fraser   I got talking to old Leon. He told me about . . . the pills.

Saskia   That's not –

Fraser   He said he found those packets –

Saskia   He –

Fraser   I told him he must have got that wrong.

He takes **Saskia***'s hand again.*

Fraser   Look, Sask, if you need help. If you need to talk to some professional then we're get the best therapist that money can buy, OK?

Saskia   No –

Fraser   No. Because I don't think you need that. I just think . . . you need a new environment. Leon's a lovely guy. But he's not . . . you.

He never had to wade through the shit. He was never hungry.

But me and you: we're the same. And I think I can make you very happy.

He leans in and kisses her.

He kisses her for a second but she pulls away.

Fraser   What do you say?

Saskia   I think . . . I think I should sign this.

. . .

Fraser   Fine . . . sign. Sure.

Saskia *takes the tablet and is about to sign . . .*

but outside the window of the Tank something catches her eye.

Her face is covered in sun and she hears children's laughter as she smiles and remembers.

Saskia (*to audience*)   . . . but outside the Tank,

through a small window I spy,

the canal, and the marshes.

And the spot . . .

Fraser   Saskia?

Saskia (*to audience*)   Where me and Dizzy,

when we were very young,

picked blackberries and stuffed them into our mouths.

Fraser   Sask?!

Saskia (*to audience*)   I can see her there. All young. And smiling . . .

but then she turns to me. I can almost see.

Her lose her smile,

And stare right up at me.

Fraser   Saskia?! Are you here? Hello.

Saskia (*to* **Fraser**)   Sorry, yes, yes.

(*To audience.*) But the contract looks all different now,

all screaming font and jagged lines . . .

Fraser   What's wrong?

Saskia   . . . Fraser.

. . . So . . . we're not gonna build . . . any council homes?

Or that park?

Fraser   . . . We want to –

Saskia   But we won't.

Fraser   Because we can't afford it.

So we grease a few palms, twist a few Brent councillors' arms. Save a few mill or two and we get it through.

Saskia   Why?

Fraser   Because we're running out of time and money and HS2 is rising out the ground like fucking acne and if we don't move, right now, those little fuckers at Keithly and Knight, those Morley Estate pricks, they would jump and it will all be gone.

And then the area will grow.

Saskia   But no council homes –

Fraser   It's just how it's done. Heygate, Nine Elms, all the bigs ones, it's just how it's done.

Saskia   But can't we do it differently . . .?

Fraser (*leaning in*)   If you don't sign this right now it will revert back to the Mayor's office –

Saskia   . . . But isn't that a good thing . . .?

Fraser   . . .

Saskia   I mean, they'll build proper homes, and parks
and –

Fraser   They'll just fuck up again. Saskia, this is the world
you are part of. This is the world you know. Stop pissing
about.

Saskia   . . .

But Fraser . . . –

Fraser   What?

Saskia   . . . don't you ever think about . . . –

What we're doing here? What we're doing to the city? The
world?

Like maybe we're . . . ripping the soul out of it.

And we'll just keep on building and building until the world
burns up in some horrible fucking mess and drowns in all
the shit we've made . . .

And before that . . . me and you . . .

we're just turning the world into one big . . . fucking Pret.

. . . Don't you ever think about that?

Fraser   . . .

. . .

Not really.

I like Pret.

He taps the tablet.

Sign it.

Saskia *holds the tablet, her hand shakes. She's pale and sick.*

Fraser   Remember, it's not just this deal. Or being partner.
It's your role with us. It's your flat. It's your life, Saskia.

It's your whole life. Everything you've built: gone.

All gone.

It's everything. Gone.

Saskia's *hand shakes above the tablet.*

As her finger hovers above the screen, about to sign, she peers out the window.

Saskia (*to audience*)   But as my quaking finger quakes above the burning screen. I look one last time out the window,

to the marshes . . .

. . . to find Dizzy gone . . . disappeared . . .

Fraser   Sign it.

Saskia (*to audience*)   She's not there . . .

*Then **Saskia** stares in horror in front of her. She thinks she sees **Dizzy**, staring at her.*

Saskia (*to audience*)   . . . She's here. She's here. In the crowd. Like Elpenor!

Staring up at me!

Fraser   Saskia?!

. . . What do you see?

Saskia   Dizzy.

Fraser   What?

Saskia   Dizzy.

Fraser   There's no one there. Sign.

Saskia (*to audience*)   He grabs my hand.

And guides it shaking, white and sick . . . to the screen.

But I feel my eyes on me . . .

Fraser   Sign it.

Saskia (*to audience*)   . . . I touch the screen.

I sign . . .

. . .

but no . . .

A scream.

Just as I'm about to I feel hellfire rise in me,

and Dizzy's eyes, burning through me,

Fraser   Saskia!

Saskia (*to audience*)   And something grim rise to the top –

Saskia *vomits violently all over the tablet.*

The whole club goes silent. They all look at **Saskia**.

Saskia (*to* **Fraser**)   Oh no, I've been sick.

Fraser   Fuck-sake.

Saskia (*wiping sick from her mouth, turning to audience*)   . . .
And then the whole club

Stops . . .

The immense shovelling of food,

of fries,

and greasy laid baskets ceases,

and everyone,

mid-mouthful,

mid-snort,

mid-gulp,

is suspended in motion. And all eyes on me. In a horrible
freeze frame of grease and white teas.

. . . But then it starts.

A scream.

The bald man, starts to weep.

The woman by the cheese plant, so sickened by me,

stops gyrating and throws up herself,

(*Sound of throwing up.*)

onto the cheese plant which then,

in spongy defiance,

then flicks back her sick over the wanton crowd.

More screams.

All hell breaks loose.

Food and screams and IPAs

and tiny dogs all leap into the air and puke and defecate on themselves and throw

all that Friday fun back up on itself!

The muscle enters:

the security guard from the door,

who howls, mid-lunge, to the air:

'Can everyone please stop throwing up!'

. . . and . . . in the vomiting crowd,

as I wipe my mouth,

I see Dizzy. Smiling at me . . .

. . . but then Fraser,

smiling too.

Calmly wiping the tablet screen,

Fraser *smiles and calmly wipes vomit from his tablet.*

Saskia   . . . Fraser?

Fraser (*smiling*)   I knew you wouldn't have the stomach for this, Sask – I didn't know how literally, but –

Saskia   What you talking about?

Fraser   . . . Leon signed for you.

Saskia   He can't do that –

Fraser   Yes he can. As your spouse, and a sharer at Eckerd and Wise, he most certainly can. Especially if you're not of right frame of mind.

Saskia   No.

Fraser   He told me about the last few months. Your friend that died. How you go out to the marshes. You talk to her –

Saskia   No –

Fraser   He said he found you in the water one night –

Saskia   I don't want to sign it. I don't want to do this! –

Fraser   . . . Well, it's done. And you'll thank me tomorrow.

Saskia (*to audience*)   . . . but then the tablet throbs in the dark . . .

(*To* **Fraser**.) . . . Wait . . . this hasn't been signed. It's a live document. I can see Leon online. He hasn't signed –

Fraser *grabs her hand.*

Fraser   But he will sign. He said he'd sign at midnight, if you don't get back, he promised me he'd sign –

Saskia   Get off me –

Fraser   He knows you're out of your mind, Sask. He'll sign anyway. You've got ten minutes, you'll never make it back!

Saskia *pushes* **Fraser** *backwards and leaps from her chair.*

Rousing, sweet string music plays, like 'The Other Side' by Michael Nyman.

Saskia (*to audience*)   . . . But I push him back

I push him down to more sick and screams.

I run from the scene,

and Dizzy, she turns, and she runs with me.

'Come on!'

she squeaks as we run

through horrible arches,

past plastic stools.

Fraser   SASKIA!

Saskia (*to audience*)   Fraser, in the glare, shouts at me. But I run . . .

Through crowds of lurching, lurching, lurching men,

Fraser   SASKIA!

Saskia (*to audience*)   **Saskia** (*to audience*)   Hurl over graffitied walls,

and down to canal,

to bridge and black water,

to sky and stars.

Fraser   SASKIA, LISTEN!

Saskia (*to audience*)   I've never seen so many stars!

Piercing through the grey growling sky . . .

Fraser   Saskia, listen!

Saskia (*to audience*)   . . . but I turn back, to see him by the bridge, silhouetted against the hazy gloom,

Fraser   Listen . . . the only difference between me and you, Saskia, is I *know* I'm a prick. And you just need to find out!

. . .

Saskia (*to audience*)   but then I feel a cool hand in mine,

'Don't listen to him.' Dizzy's eyes sparkle and she points east,

to the dusty path,

where the road splits,

and the marshes . . .

to that road we took so many years ago,

where we ran and ran and ran,

Down dusty path,

to straggled trees,

to woods and tangled dark,

To save the day!

Her smart watch rings but she doesn't notice at first.

To make things right,

and Dizzy,

she seems to glide, her dress flowing like bubbling waves

above tangled slipways, she glides,

she soars, she rises to the stars!

Guiding me through the marsh,

and trees covered in crisp packets,

and sweet wrappers,

like Christmas.

And suddenly I'm in love . . . with this beautiful, horrible city,

this terrible beautiful place.

This everything at once.

She notices her smart watch ringing and answers it.

It's **Leon**.

Leon (*phone call*)   Saskia, Saskia?!

Saskia   Leon . . .

Leon   Where are you?!

Saskia   I'm on the marsh, Leon, it's so beautiful –

Leon   Don't do anything, stay where you are, don't go near the lake . . . –

Suddenly, **Saskia** *trips and falls squarely in the mud. She remembers this place with horror.*

The music continues but more melancholic. Sunlight pours in, a memory begins:

Saskia (*to audience*)   . . . but too late . . .

I fall on some knotted, gnarled root . . .

my hand slips out of Dizzy's . . . just like it did all those years ago . . .

this place . . . this little patch of heath,

with barbed wire,

and peat –

stinking soil –

where Dizzy stood, all those years ago.

Saskia   No!

(*To audience.*) I try to pull her back, just like I did back then.

But she stares ahead, defiantly.

Sounds of cackling laughter and people surrounding.

And suddenly, silhouetted, shadowed,

hyena cackling, cider-ed up,

angry, horny, bored, bitter, battery-acid mean.

Teens, kids. Gather round. And pick at her hair.

'Oi, it's the freak!'

Shanice Lane is first to say, prowling from the pack,

'Why you here, freak?!'

Melissa Brown speaks, and everyone laughs, teeanged faced and

laughing-gas wild.

But Dizzy stands there defiant and says, clear as day:

'We want to come to the party.'

The whole crowd erupts, with honks and hoots and closing in.

'We?' Shanice Lane utters up,

and looks at me,

'What? Saskia? Is she your friend . . .? Are you friends with the freak?'

. . . everyone goes quiet. Dizzy looks at me.

. . .

And then Dizzy says.

'Yes, she's my friend.'

. . . The crowd erupts again. Shanice's eyes narrow, all lizard-like and daggered,

Melissa Brown wets herself with cruel

peels of laughter.

'Is that true, Sask? Are you friends with this fucking freak?'

. . .

All eyes on me.

. . . Dizzy stares . . .

. . .

'No,'

I say simple and Shanice, she smiles.

'Good'

and then, with two metal rings on her fist,

punches Dizzy hard across the mouth.

The crowd around erupts,

'Oh, man, that's deep'

half laughing, half shudders,

as Shanice leans into Dizzy, half on the ground,

and whispers, 'See, I told you I'd get you back.'

And in my mind I'm screaming,

'No, Dizzy, no!'

as Dizzy gathers foam in her mouth,

and lifts her silent face up,

and gobs Shanice Lane right in the face!

'OOOOOHHH!!' shout the boys and girls again,

stunned,

electrified,

amazed at what they have just seen.

'She done you, Shanice! She merked you right there in the face.'

And even though, amazed, Shanice Lane turned back,

and barked at Melissa Brown, still stony shocked:

'Grab her arms.'

And Melissa, although slow at first, did. And even though
Dizzy spat, and struggled,

and struck out,

(*Sound of slapping, which merges with the lightning back on the real
marsh, in present times.* **Saskia** *shudders with each slap.*)

the coward Melissa held her firm,

and pushed her down, as Shanice

punch and tore at Dizzy's face with metal rings,

and the burnt earth was speckled,

with blood.

And the crowd, at first ecstatic, grew silent,

and sick, and shuddered with each metal slap . . .

But I wouldn't know . . .

. . .

I am told Chris Hutton, arriving late, broke it up.

'Oi, leave her alone, man!' dragging Shanice Lane off her
prey,

but I wouldn't know . . .

because I . . .

. . . I had already walked away.

The sunlight disappears. The memory ends.

*Thunder and lightning crack above her and it starts to rain,
increasingly.*

Saskia *lies face down in the mud, back in the present. She looks out
at the lake nearby and moves towards the bank.*

*The string music, like Michael Nyman's 'The Other Side', plays but
less energetic, sad.*

We never spoke again after that, Dizzy and me.

After a few weeks she came back into school,

her face still bruised, and quietly sat her exams,

and of course did quite well,

And passed me in the hall,

like a ghost.

And as my life got shitter,

I watched hers grow: first Facebook, then the Gram.

I watched a shiny life of books,

and parties,

and little trips,

with friends and ideas blooming over candle-lit dinners: a life well-lived.

. . . but then, as my life started to improve,

her Gram got nastier,

more opaque. More ranty, less friends . . .

and after I began to forget,

I heard one summer, when she returned, someone saw her, here,

muttering by the lake.

And when I began to soar, I heard she she dropped out, of uni,

And lived back with her mum. Whose brain had started to go as well.

And Dizzy was seen out there again, by the lake.

And just as

. . . and then I heard.

From Melissa Brown of all people, Shanice's right hand.
Now the manager of our local Boots.

'. . . Did you hear about Dizzy? . . . That's fucked, you kna.

I feel deep . . .'

. . . apparently,

a dog-walker had been running here one dawn,

and in the purple water saw,

Dizzy.

Her hair, curling up with reeds,

and the coroner later agreed,

her body was full of pills.

But, as the dog-walker said,

her green eyes were wide open,

and shone sunlight in the morning breeze.

. . .

. . .

And a few nights before she called me . . .

she basically told me she was gonna do it. I pretended not to
understand but . . . I could have stopped her . . .

. . .

And then, after that, like a curse from the Fates.

Everything fell to bits.

The panic attacks, the staring at the walls,

the dreams . . .

the calls . . .

I heard her voice, on the marsh, calling me.

I could almost see her, in the water,

hand outstretched. On this very spot. Calling me.

'Saskia.'

Saskia *stands at the lake, face covered in green and blue, reflected from the water. She sees* **Dizzy** *staring up at her from the water.*

. . . and there she is now.

Down there in the water.

hand outstretched,

'Saskia.'

black hair, and reeds, curling up.

. . . and she's smiling,

'Saskia'

she calling me . . .

and now . . . I must pick up.

Lightning flashes and thunder.

Thunder cracks above Stratford,

slashing it apart like some alien ship.

A bell tower chimes: midnight.

Somewhere though, from some last wooded bit of east,

some last bit the cranes didn't pick,

. . . a church bell chimes, I didn't know they still did that . . .

It chimes long and slow, it chimes midnight.

Well that makes things easier.

The contract's. Gone.

Too late anyway, to save the day. And on the horizon, I even see . . . that white bird again . . .

fly away from me . . . .

'So, come join me anyway.'

Whispers Dizzy, all whispery and weeping willowed,

down in the dark, dark,

dark, water.

Why not?

Lightning flashes, again and again.

A long, long sleep for Saskia Dunne.

Leon *runs in from the trees as* **Saskia** *is about to jump into the water. She does not hear him.*

Saskia (*to audience*)   Coward.

Loser.

Leon   SASKIA!

Saskia (*to audience*)   Queen of the scum.

Right at the end of her stupid little run.

Leon   SASKIA!

Saskia (*to audience*)   'Saskia'

whispers Dizzy,

one last time.

Leon   NOO!

Saskia (*to audience*)   And in I go.

As **Leon** *makes to stop her by dragging her down,*

Saskia *jumps into the water.*

Lightning crashes and thunder rolls.

She leaps into the black water,

and all air and sound is extinguished as she drowns.

Lightning above her ripples,

screams and shouts from **Leon** *and other voices.*

But everything fades to black as **Saskia***'s body at first struggles and tries to swim back upwards.*

But she can't and her body goes limp.

Everything fades as her body stops moving.

There is a last tiny glow around her face.

As she dies, **Saskia** *remembers the phone call that she had from* **Dizzy***, a few months before.*

The string music, like Michael Nyman's 'The Other Side', carries on but even sadder and lighter.

The sound of a phone ringing and then picked up by **Saskia***.*

Dizzy   . . . Saskia? Can you hear me?

Saskia   . . .

Dizzy   Saskia.

Saskia   . . .

Dizzy   It's Dizzy. From school, do you –

Saskia   Of course I do . . .

It's . . . so good to hear your voice. So . . . –

Dizzy   Are you OK?

Saskia   Yeah, just a little drunk. We landed the biggest deal of my career tonight.

Dizzy   Congratulations.

Saskia   . . .

Saskia   You know it's crazy, Diz. I'm at my flat and I'm looking at the marsh and I'm thinking of you and then . . . you call . . . –

Dizzy   Saskia –

Saskia   You don't understand what I'd do to change that day. You don't –

Dizzy   . . . Saskia. I'm not calling about that. I'm not angry about that anymore, I'm just . . . leaving.

Saskia   What?

Dizzy   I'm leaving the area.

Saskia   . . . where you going?

Dizzy   . . . I just wanted to know if you were OK.

Saskia   . . . Me?

Dizzy   . . . Cos first I was angry with you. Then I forgot. And then I felt . . . sorry.

Saskia   . . . Sorry?

Dizzy   I thought, you know: I'm a wreck but at least I know. But Saskia,

She must be the saddest girl in the world. And she doesn't even know it.

Saskia *nods her head slowly, crying, in agreement.*

Dizzy   . . . but it's good to know you're happy.

Saskia   I'm not happy. I haven't been happy since . . . that day, on the canal. That was the happiest day of my life.

Dizzy   . . . Me too.

Saskia   . . .?

Dizzy   I have to go.

Saskia   Please don't go, please don't go.

Dizzy   Saskia – whatever happens to me.

Saskia   No –

Dizzy   It's not cos of you. I just didn't make it. Some of us don't make it.

Saskia   No, Dizzy –

Dizzy   The only one you ever harmed was yourself, Saskia. Again and again.

Saskia   . . .

Saskia   . . . But this life . . . this fucking horrible life it's taken hold of me. It's wrapped me up, I can't get out –

Dizzy   There's always something you can do.

Saskia   So can you –

Dizzy   No! No . . . I'm done. But you. You could be happy. But you have to be unhappy too.

Saskia   . . .

Dizzy   . . . Let it in.

Saskia   What?

Dizzy   Let in all the darkness. And the shit. And the bad stuff. You have to let it in.

Saskia   . . .

Dizzy   Let it in, cos if you don't, it will kill you.

Saskia   . . .

Dizzy   Let it in, and live with it. Live with both. Like I never could . . . but you can.

Having lain limp, **Saskia***'s body convulses in the water as a few bubbles escape her mouth.*

The string music, like Michael Nyman's 'The Other Side', gathers momentum and builds and builds: less sad, more triumphant as **Saskia** *swims to the top.*

Saskia (*to audience*)   Above me . . .

Saskia   . . . I want to live.

Dizzy   What?

Saskia   I want to live . . .

Saskia (*to audience*)   Above me . . .

Dizzy   . . . So show me.

Show me, Saskia.

Saskia*'s body convulses again as more bubbles escape her mouth and her eyes jump open.*

Leon*'s hand thrusts into the water, searching for* **Saskia***.*

Saskia (*to audience*)   Above me. Thunder. Shouts,

black lighting rolling,

rippling across . . .

Dizzy   Show me, Saskia –

can't breathe.

Breathe.

Saskia   Can't move.

Dizzy   Move.

Saskia   Can't . . . see . . .

Dizzy *helps to pull her to swim upwards.*

Dizzy   Come on! Remember . . . Brighton! Yeah, and, and . . . Paris! And move, that 10K in Fife!

Saskia   . . .

Leon *can be heard shouting at the top.*

Saskia   And look, Leon! There, at the top! Remember . . . night-lamps, and chats, and . . .

Saskia   . . . Remember Dizzy.

Dizzy   Yeah, remember me! And . . . bruised knees,

Saskia   and apples trees!

Dizzy   And water like honey.

Saskia *looks around.*

Saskia (*to audience*)   And in the water now, there are smiles. Smiling at me.

Delroy *enters, the man from the beginning.*

Delroy, **Kerry** *and* **Lottie** *can physically enter or their voices performed.* **Saskia**'*s swimming improves as they speak and she thrusts upwards.*

Their voices are drowned out as the music and thunder intensify.

Delroy   Remember me.

Saskia (*to audience*)   Delroy. The man on the bench.

Delroy   Remember Meanwhile.

Saskia   . . . The Gardens!

Delroy   And the Westway soaring west!

Kerry *enters, the Lidl lady.*

Kerry   And remember me!

Saskia   Kerry!

Kerry   And Mudchute, and Ridley Road! And the battles yet to come.

Saskia   Remember.

Lottie *enters, the canal boat lady.*

Lottie   And remember, Saskia.

Saskia   . . .

Lottie   Find what makes you happy. Find what makes you happy. And hold on to it.

Saskia   . . . hold on.

Lottie   And Remember.

Kerry   Remember.

Delroy   Remember.

Lottie   Remember.

Dizzy   And up, up, up, we go!

Saskia *swims and swims,*

surging up to the top of dark water.

She just manages to grab **Leon***'s hand and, as his hand grips hers,*

she pierces through the water.

She is pulled up, wide-eyed, and gasping for air, onto the

muddy bank in Hackney Marshes

as the storm subsides and she lies, panting and coughing up water,

and **Leon** *holds her and moves her hair from her face, looking into*
her eyes.

Other people also help her out of the water.

The music continues, but lighter, and there are shouts around her.

Leon   Saskia?! Saskia?!

Saskia *coughs up more water as* **Leon** *holds her. She falls back on*
the bank and stares up at the stars. She is a daze throughout.

Leon   Give her some room!

Saskia (*to audience*)   . . . purple bank.

Leon   Saskia?

Saskia (*to audience*)   . . . tree . . . purple sky . . . storm
subsides . . .

Leon   Saskia, look at me. Can you see me.

Saskia (*to audience*)   and marshes, spreading out and liquid sky and rumbling away

Saskia (*to* **Leon**)   Leon . . .

Leon   Oh, Saskia, Sask.

Saskia   Leon.

They kiss and hold each other.

Saskia   I'm so sorry . . . about everything.

Leon   . . . it's OK. (*Calling out.*) I think she's OK.

Saskia (*to audience*)   There are others on the purple bank, figures flicking with the reeds.

A man, I know . . .

Saskia   Chris?

(*To audience.*) Chris Hutton stands there, reeds in his hands from dragging me up.

Leon   . . . he came up here when you ran out of the pub, he wanted to see if you –

Saskia   Thank you.

(*To audience.*) He nods and smiles at me. And beside him . . . in her nightie . . . –

Saskia   Mum?

(*To audience.*) Looking smaller and . . . older. Face tear-stained gold.

She bends to me as Chris clears his throat.

Chris   I grabbed her when you ran out the pub. She said she thought you would be here . . . –

Saskia   It's alright, Mum.

Mum   No, it's not. Listen, Sask. It was never you I hated. It was him. Your Dad. Just cos . . . he left and . . . you reminded me . . . of –

Saskia   It's OK, Mum.

Mum   I just didn't want you to be a loser . . . like me . . .

but you do what makes you happy, OK? Whatever that is. You do what makes you happy.

Saskia   OK Mum, OK.

Fraser

Saskia (*to audience*)   another shout, this time from our flat,

A white starchy shirt cuts the dark,

suddenly there is after-shave, and teeth.

Fraser *enters, out of breath and still holding the tablet with contract.*

Fraser   Saskia. Thank. God.

Saskia (*to audience*)   Fraser. He bends down, doing his best Hollywood.

Fraser   Oh God, I'm so glad you're OK. So glad.

Saskia (*to audience*)   Leon bristles, but then his hand goes a little limp in mine.

Fraser takes my hand, as Chris and Mum stand back.

Saskia   Wait, Mum, no –

Fraser   Sask . . . I'm so sorry. I didn't listen . . . we're gonna get you the best help money can buy. We have counsellors at Eckerd and Wise –

Saskia   No! . . . Not from you.

Fraser   . . . OK. We'll get someone external . . . –

Leon   Do you have the contract?

Saskia (*to audience*)   Leon says, whilst stroking my hair.

Fraser   Yeah, did you sign?

Leon   Sure.

Fraser *takes the tablet still in his hands and scrolls through the contract, to find the signature.*

Saskia   Leon . . .? No –

Fraser   Babe, listen. I know this doesn't –

Saskia   No –

Fraser   I know this doesn't feel right right now but tomorrow morning. It will just be like a bad dream.

Saskia   Leon –

Fraser   We're doing this for you.

Leon   He's right, Sask.

Saskia (*to audience*)   Leon looks down and grips my hand and smiles. Fraser gets to the bottom of the doc and frowns:

Leon   Wait, Leon, mate, you've got this wrong. You haven't put your name . . . you've written. Wa . . . wet . . . ben? Wet – Ben?

Leon   No, it says 'Wet Bag'.

Fraser   . . .

Leon   That's what I am, isn't it?

Fraser   I don't think that will hold up in a court of law.

Saskia   Leon –

She smiles up at **Leon** *as* **Leon** *stands.*

Leon   Well, I guess you'll just have to do something extra illegal, won't you.

Fraser   Do you understand what you've done?

. . . you've fucked up our lives, do you understand? You fucking idiot!

Leon   Saskia didn't want it.

Fraser   Saskia's two ticks from the nuthouse, you fucking mug! This is everything we've fucking built, this is everything.

He pushes **Leon**.

Saskia   Leon.

Fraser *bends down to* **Saskia**.

Fraser   Listen, Sask. Listen. There's still a way we can fix this.

Saskia   . . .

Fraser   If you get behind this wholeheartedly, there's still a way we can get new contracts –

Saskia   No!

I don't want to, Fraser. I don't want to do this anymore.

Fraser   . . . Saskia, it's not just you, it's me, it's the whole company.

Leon   Stop –

Fraser   It's this flat, it's your life: gone.

Leon   Leave her alone!

Fraser *presses his forehead against* **Leon**.

Fraser   And what the fuck are you gonna do? Hmm? You little drip.

Chris   Easy.

Saskia (*to audience*)   Chris says from the back. But Fraser pushes

Leon, again and again,

Fraser   What are you gonna do about it?

Saskia   Leave him alone! –

Fraser   What you gonna do!

Leon *hesitates but then headbutts* **Fraser** *squarely in the face.*

Fraser*, shocked, staggers back and holds his bloodied nose.*

Fraser   Headbutt?! . . . Who the fuck headbutts?

Saskia (*to audience*)   But when he throws himself back at Leon,

big Chris Hutton stands in the way, blocking Fraser's pathetic fists.

Chris   You're done, bruv. You're done.

And helps him walk away,

but Fraser hurls back, as his white shirt disappears:

Fraser   I'm done?! You're done, all of you are fucking done! I'll build a fucking car park on your swamp, I'll block up the canal, I'll build a Pret on the fucking moon! I will build my fucking city, you just wait. You just fucking wait.

Saskia (*to audience*)   But Chris takes him away . . .

and Mum shuffles off too.

Mum   I'll leave you two.

And then we are alone.

. . .

and the sky above us,

above the marsh is pink with a little morning.

I lean in to him.

Leon *sits with* **Saskia** *and she lies back against him.*

Leon   Saskia.

Saskia   Yes?

Leon   You know we're totally screwed, yeah? We'll be homeless.

Saskia   Yes.

Leon   Jobless.

Saskia   Yes.

Leon   Poor.

Saskia   Yes!

She laughs and smiles at him. They look out across the marsh at the trees towards the west.

A large bird is heard calling.

Saskia (*to audience*)   Out on the marshes, the sky is pink, and getting pinker,

there are trees now as the shadows disappear and sun slips between them and,

and above that: the city.

Leon   What do you want now?

Saskia (*to audience*)   Leon whispers in my ear as we face it all,

Saskia   I want to go to sleep . . . then I want to wake up.

And then I want to take Rosa. And go somewhere.

Leon   Where?

Saskia (*to audience*)   And as I lean into him,

above the scraggy trees, something flashes white,

Saskia (*to* **Leon**)   Look!

(*To audience.*) It glistens and glides and takes off over Stratford,

and the A12 flying by.

Saskia   Look!

Leon   Oh yeah, that bird!

Saskia (*to audience*)   Dizzy . . .

She circles round,

the clouds of trees,

and extends its winds and seems to look at me and flies above our heads,

(*To* **Leon**.) Look, look!

(*To audience*.) And then, with one broad sweep, it turns from Stratford, burning in the east,

and heads back west.

over Hackney Wick,

Victoria Park,

and beyond!

It flies straight and clear,

back along the canal,

through Dalston,

Camden,

Kensal Green,

and then Park Royal,

Old Oak . . .

to stay there,

and watch over.

Leon   It's flying away . . .

Saskia *watches the bird fly away. She turns to audience.*

Saskia (*to audience*)   . . .

And watch over, with her.

All of us.

. . . Look to the north.

Look to the south.

Look to the east.

Look to the west.

And . . . and hold on.

And protect.

What you love.

. . . And what is left.

The sun brightens

as the birdsong

and music reach a crescendo,

before gently

fading

away.

. . .

The End.

Printed in the USA
CPSIA information can be obtained
at www.ICGtesting.com
LVHW020108181123
764246LV00002B/380